Innovations in Disaster and
Trauma Psychology
Volume Two:

Critical Incident Stress Management

- CISM -

A New Era and Standard of Care in Crisis Intervention

Innovations in Disaster and
Trauma Psychology
Volume Two:

Critical Incident Stress Management

- CISM -

A New Era and Standard of Care in Crisis Intervention

George S. Everly, Jr., Ph.D., F.A.P.M.
and
Jeffrey T. Mitchell, Ph.D.

Chevron Publishing Corporation ◆ Ellicott City, MD

Editorial / Production Supervision and Interior Design:
Dana M. Fuller, B.A.

Front and Back Cover Design:
Dana M. Fuller, B.A.
Caroline J. Zimmerman, B.A.

Cover photograph donated by:
Jeffrey T. Mitchell, Ph.D.

Chevron Publishing Corporation
5018 Dorsey Hall Drive
Suite 104
Ellicott City, MD 21042
(410) 740 - 0065

Printed in the United States of America

Dedications

To my family - the joy in my life (GSE)

Dedicated to my mother, Rita, and my sister, June, who have
done so much to alleviate human suffering (JTM)

Preface

This volume represents a new era in crisis intervention. It is the first book ever written on Critical Incident Stress Management (CISM) as a comprehensive crisis response program. By comprehensive, we mean an integrated, multicomponent intervention system that spans the entire crisis spectrum from pre-crisis preparation and on-scene support services through post-crisis intervention and follow-up mental health dispensations, as necessary. The comprehensive nature of the CISM formulation finds its historical roots in the work of Gerald Caplan (1964, 1969) who proposed the notions of primary, secondary, and tertiary prevention. And that is, indeed, the essence of this volume. That is, CISM is a programmatic approach to reducing the frequency, duration, severity of, and impairment from, psychological crises.

Acknowledgments

Few contributions to the human condition occur in isolation. Human beings depend upon one another. They share their ideas, their wisdom, their vision and their support for one another. A final product most often depends upon an intricate interrelationship between people who share the same spirit and life orientation.

The final product represented by this book attests to the productivity which can be achieved when people share their very best with others. This book could never have been written without the cooperation of many. Yes, the authors wrote the words, but the refinements to ideas came about as a result of the sharing of many.

The traumatized should be the first to be thanked. It was their intimate experiences with trauma that form the background against which this volume was written. They have in the past, and continue now, to teach us things which can be useful to others. They have learned the lessons of trauma well and they have taught us those same lessons in turn. Thank you to all of you who have had the courage to speak freely about your pain. Others owe you a great debt. Their footsteps in traumatic stress are made easier because you have provided a map to recovery.

The next groups which should be credited with a contribution to this volume are the over four hundred Critical Incident Stress Management teams which operate in 19 nations. Not only have they given generously of their talents and energies to mitigate human suffering and restore people to normal function, they have also provided a constant stream of feedback regarding CISM services. Their advice and support have been instrumental in the development of this volume and in many other ways. It is impossible to list each one individually. There are simply too many of you. But your contributions, both small and great, are deeply appreciated. You do make a difference in the lives of others.

Next, we are grateful to our families who have tolerated long periods of our absence so that the work of Critical Incident Stress Management could make progress. Their support gives us the strength to achieve works such as this book.

Finally, we would be remiss if we did not acknowledge the small, but efficient staff of Chevron Publishing, especially Caroline Zimmerman and Dana Fuller who worked tirelessly to produce this volume on incredibly short notice. Thanks for your professionalism.

To each of you, who has become part of the fabric of our lives, we express our gratitude. We wish you the best of all good things.

Sincerely,

George S. Everly, Jr., Ph.D.   Jeffrey T. Mitchell, Ph.D.
March, 1997

Table of Contents

CHAPTER FOUR:

CHAPTER FIVE:

CHAPTER SIX:

CHAPTER SEVEN:

CHAPTER ONE

Foundations of Crisis Intervention and Critical Incident Stress Management

One can hardly pick up a daily newspaper or weekly magazine without reading about crisis, crime, violence, or mass disaster. From its first landmark case in August of 1986 when 13 postal workers were shot to death on the job in Oklahoma, violence in the workplace has become a virtual epidemic, a plague on society that has no practical remedy in the foreseeable future. Such violence not only sends psychological shockwaves through the businesses and communities wherein they occur, but it plants and nurtures the seeds of distrust, anxiety, social paranoia, and even defensive aggression. In the last decade, we have similarly been rudely awakened to the psychological legacy of social catastrophe, mass disaster, and war. In response, the American Red Cross and the American Psychological Association created a bold initiative to provide mental health services in the wake of disaster. But prior even to this initiative, the International Critical Incident Stress Foundation, Inc. was providing training and consultation services designed to mitigate work-related stress amongst the emergency services professions, such as fire suppression, law enforcement, prehospital medical services, search and rescue, disaster relief and the like. As the recognition of the vast need to provide crisis and disaster mental health services has grown, so too has there been an emergence, if not renaissance, in the provision of such mental health services. The purpose of this volume is to offer a new integrative and comprehensive paradigm for the provision of crisis response and disaster mental health services. It is hoped that such a paradigm will not only serve to advance the field of crisis and disaster mental health, but will serve as a viable standard of care in crisis intervention for the new millennium. We have called this new paradigm for the delivery of crisis and disaster mental health services, Critical Incident Stress Management (CISM).

In the remaining pages of this chapter, we shall discuss the foundations of the emergency provision of psychological services. We shall do so by examining two distinct epochs, or generations, in the evolution of crisis intervention.

EPOCH ONE: HISTORICAL ROOTS OF CRISIS INTERVENTION

From a historical perspective, the provision of emergency psychological care has most often been referred to as crisis intervention. Indeed, crisis intervention is sometimes thought of as "emotional first-aid" (Neil, Oney, DiFonso, Thacker, and Reichart, 1974).

In order to better understand the nature of crisis intervention, let us first offer a working definition of a psychological crisis. As the body struggles to maintain a physical homeostasis, or "steady state," so the mind struggles to maintain a similar balance. A psychological crisis represents a condition wherein the individual's psychological balance has been disrupted, there is, in effect, a psychological disequilibrium. More practically speaking, a crisis may be defined as a state wherein one's usual coping mechanisms have failed in the face of a perceived challenge or threat. Caplan (1969) denoted two types of crises:

1) developmental, and 2) situational. Symptoms of a crisis condition may include:

1) a range of affective presentations from panic to depression,
2) cognitive dysfunctions,
3) the presentation of a wide variety of physical complaints, and / or
4) irratic, or maladaptive behavior.

Crisis - a temporary condition wherein one's usual coping mechanisms have failed in the face of a perceived challenge or threat

---

Having noted the nature of a crisis, the goals of crisis intervention become more apparent. Most simply stated, the goals of crisis intervention should include assisting the person in crisis to return to a more "steady state" of psychological functioning (i.e., psychological homeostasis). Practically speaking, the goal of crisis intervention is to assist the person in returning to an adaptive level of independent functioning that approximates the pre-crisis level of adaptation (Parad, 1996; Neil, Oney, DiFonso, Thacker, and Reichart, 1974; Caplan, 1964).

The focus of the intervention is always the present crisis condition as opposed to past crises and / or chronic contributing factors.

Crisis Intervention - Emotional "first aid" designed to assist the person in crisis in returning to independent functioning

---

Historically, interest in crisis intervention may be rooted in, and seen as a natural corollary to, investigations into the psychological consequences of crisis and disaster. Among the first of the systematic inquiries into disaster psychology was the work of Edward Stierlin (1909) who investigated the psychological aftermath of a major European mining disaster in 1906. Later, T.W. Salmon made a significant contribution to the literature via his recollections and analyses of psychiatric emergencies during World War I. From his work, and that of Kardiner and Spiegel (1947), the three principles of crisis intervention - immediacy, proximity, and expectancy - were derived.

Many modern writers point to Eric Lindemann's (1944) account of the November 28, 1943 Coconut Grove night club fire in Boston, wherein 492 people lost their lives, as the beginning of modern crisis intervention theory and practice. Lindemann was later joined by Gerald Caplan in the creation of a community mental health program which emphasized community outreach and crisis intervention in the Boston metropolitan area.

Another important development in the early modern era of crisis intervention was the work of suicidologists Edwin Schneidman and Norman Farberow. In the mid 1950s, they created the prototype for suicide prevention centers in the United States in the form of the Los Angeles Suicide Prevention Center.

The field of crisis intervention received a major boost when in 1963 President John Kennedy called for a "bold new approach" to the delivery of mental health services. The national Community Mental Health Centers' Act was the result of that appeal. This congressional act established a network of community based mental health service centers wherein a major emphasis was placed upon crisis intervention services as a form of preventive outreach.

The 1960s and 1970s saw a proliferation of walk-in clinics

and telephone hotlines. Clearly the heyday of fundamental crisis intervention services, this "first epoch" in community crisis intervention saw the following **advances**:

1) the provision of services within a prevention framework (Caplan, 1964),
2) deinstitutionalization of psychiatric services,
3) aggressive community outreach,
4) emphasis on crisis intervention services as a viable mental health delivery paradigm, and
5) the use of paraprofessional counselors trained in nondirective, client-centered counseling interventions.

The primary **delivery systems** during this "first epoch" in community crisis intervention were:

1) walk-in clinics and
2) telephone hotlines.

The primary crisis **intervention technologies** employed during this "first epoch" in community crisis intervention were:

1) nondirective, client-centered counseling and
2) basic problem solving and conflict resolution techniques.

As the 1970s drew to a close and we progressed through the 1980s, enthusiasm in crisis intervention services seemed to wane. Thus, the first epoch in the history of crisis intervention drew to a close.

EPOCH TWO: HISTORICAL ROOTS OF CRITICAL INCIDENT STRESS MANAGEMENT (CISM)

As we look toward a new millennium, we stand well entrenched in a renaissance of crisis intervention. The scope of intervention delivery systems has broadened as have the intervention tactics. Even some of the basic terminology has changed. So different is the renaissance in crisis intervention that we believe that it truly represents a new epoch in the evolution of this discipline's theory and practice. This second epoch will be referred to as Critical Incident Stress Management (CISM) and represents a "new" integrative and comprehensive paradigm for the provision of crisis and disaster mental health services. Let's begin with the basics.

The term "critical incident" was actually borrowed not from emergency psychiatry, but from the field of organizational behavior. Flanagan (1954) proposed a method for job analysis which was referred to as the "critical incident technique." Workers were instructed to keep a diary, of sorts, which catalogued specific behaviors which were most associated with successful, as well as, unsuccessful job outcomes. These "critical incidents" were believed to be powerful predictors of success or failure on the job, hence their importance.

Mitchell and Everly (1996) have defined a critical incident as any event that can exert such a stressful impact so as to overwhelm an individual's usual coping mechanisms. Thus, by definition a critical incident is, indeed, a crisis event, sometimes thought of as a traumatic event.

Critical Incident - a crisis event which can overwhelm one's usual coping mechanisms

---

The natural corollary of the critical incident is Critical Incident Stress Management (CISM). As defined by Mitchell and Everly (1996) Critical Incident Stress Management represents an integrative, comprehensive programmatic approach to the prevention and mitigation of critical incident (traumatic) stress.

The CISM formulation is remarkably consistent with Caplan's (1964) formulations of:

1) primary prevention (i.e., the identification and mitigation of pathogenic stressors);

2) secondary prevention (i.e., the identification and mitigation of dysfunctional symptom patterns), and

3) tertiary prevention (i.e., follow-up mental health services).

Thus, the specific goals of the CISM program are:

- To reduce the:
  1) incidence,
  2) duration,
  3) severity of, or
  4) impairment from, traumatic stress arising from crisis situations, and

- To facilitate follow-up mental health interventions, when necessary.

Primary Prevention - reducing stressors and promoting health to reduce the incidence of mental illness
Secondary Prevention - mitigation of mental dysfunction through early intervention
Tertiary Prevention - follow-up mental health services

The origins of CISM, as we know it today, can be found in the writings of Jeffrey T. Mitchell (1983a, 1983b) and Christine Dunning (1988) in the United States, as well as Beverly Raphael (1986) in Australia.

The most prolific of these pioneers has been Mitchell (1988a, 1988b; Mitchell and Everly, 1996). In the mid 1970s, Mitchell became aware of the need to provide crisis intervention services to the emergency services professions (law enforcement, fire suppression, emergency medical services) due to their unique occupationally-driven vulnerability to traumatic stress disorders. But Mitchell was also aware that crisis intervention services, as they had been historically provided, would be of limited value to these professional groups. As a result, Mitchell began to reformulate, in a far more integrated and comprehensive manner, the delivery of crisis intervention services (Mitchell and Everly, 1996).

The CISM concept has been utilized not only in traditional emergency services such as law enforcement, fire suppression, and paramedicine (Fernandez, 1994; Everly, 1995b; Solomon, 1995; Kennedy-Ewing, 1988; Robinson, 1995; van Goethem, 1989; Mitchell and Everly, 1993); but also with:

- healthcare systems (Spitzer and Burke, 1993; Welzant, Torpey, and Sienkilewski, 1995),
- psychiatric hospitals (Flannery, et al., 1995),
- rescue and disaster personnel (Armstrong, O'Callahan, and Marmar, 1991; Everly, 1995a; Myers, 1995),
- nursing personnel (Kirwan, 1994; Western Management Consultants, 1996),
- jurors (Feldman and Bell, 1991),
- bank personnel (Manton and Talbot, 1990; Talbot, Manton, and Dunn, 1992),
- the airline industry (Martinez, 1995),
- military personnel (Rayner, 1994; Meehan, 1996; U.S. Air Force, 1996), and even
- an entire community devastated by natural disaster (Everly, Mitchell, and Schiller, 1995).

In addition, CISM services have been adopted by educational systems (especially colleges), water safety organizations, and numerous employee assistance programs (EAPs) serving a wide variety of businesses and industrial organizations.

In the evolution of crisis intervention services, Epoch Two, that is, Critical Incident Stress Management (CISM) represents *advances* beyond previous applications in that CISM represents an integrated, comprehensive (covering the complete crisis continuum from pre-crisis through follow-up services) program of intervention services. Its comprehensive nature gives it the flexibility to be applied to a wide diversity of settings and constituent groups.

The primary **delivery systems** in CISM are:

1. Pre-crisis preparedness training venues,
2. On-scene (the crisis venue itself),
3. Collateral crisis venues, or pericrisis venues, and
4. Post-crisis venues.

The primary **intervention technologies** of CISM are the seven integrated components enumerated in Table 1.1 below.

Table 1.1

A Comprehensive CISM Program

1. Pre-crisis preparedness training
2. One-on-one, individual psychological support
   (1 to 3 sessions)
3. Demobilizations
4. Defusings
5. Critical Incident Stress Debriefings (CISD)
6. Family support programs
7. Referral mechanisms for mental health
   assessment and possible treatment,
   if needed.

Each of the 7 CISM components enumerated in Table 1.1 will be described in greater detail later in this volume.

A STANDARD OF CARE

The concept of "standard of care" is an important one to anyone dedicated to the improvement of the human condition. Very simply stated, the term "standard of care" refers to a generally recognized and accepted procedure, intervention, or pattern of practice. Once acknowledged, interventions considered within the framework of a standard of care serve to set the minimal expectations for service provision.

CRITICAL INCIDENT STRESS MANAGEMENT (CISM) AS A STANDARD OF CARE IN CRISIS INTERVENTION

This volume presents the core concepts of CISM for consideration as a new standard of care within the context of crisis intervention services. The proposal is a simple one, that is, that crisis intervention services be conceived of as, and implemented within, a multicomponent integrated program of services that span the full crisis spectrum from pre-crisis preparation and on-scene support, through post-crisis intervention and referral for formal mental health assessment and treatment (Everly, 1997).

The integrated, multicomponent CISM system is depicted on the next page against a critical incident crisis timeline in Figure 1.1.

Scrutiny of Figure 1.1 reveals that the seven core CISM interventions have been superimposed upon a critical incident timeline.

I. The first intervention labelled "pre-incident preparation" occurs in the pre-crisis phase. The goals of pre-incident preparation are to set the appropriate expectancies for personnel as to the nature of the crisis and trauma risk factors they face. The corollary of this expectancy is to teach basic crisis coping skills in a proactive manner.

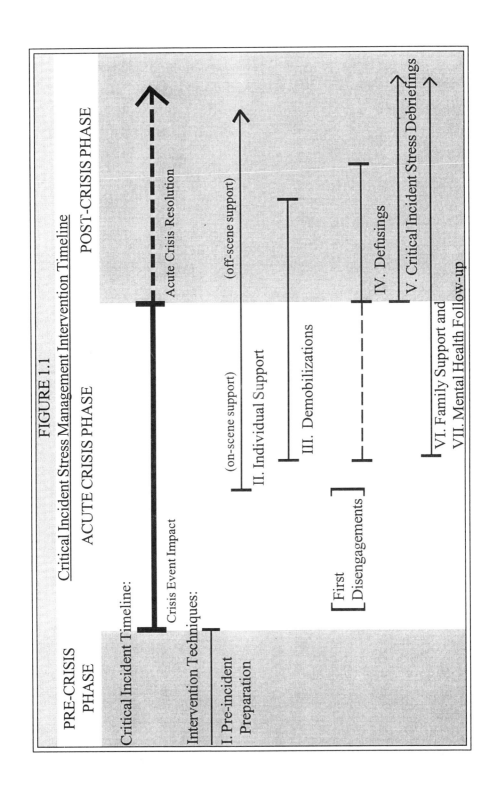

FIGURE 1.1
Critical Incident Stress Management Intervention Timeline

PRE-CRISIS PHASE   ACUTE CRISIS PHASE   POST-CRISIS PHASE

Critical Incident Timeline:

Crisis Event Impact

Acute Crisis Resolution

Intervention Techniques:

I. Pre-incident Preparation

[First Disengagements]

(on-scene support)
II. Individual Support
(off-scene support)

III. Demobilizations

IV. Defusings

V. Critical Incident Stress Debriefings

VI. Family Support and
VII. Mental Health Follow-up

As we enter the acute crisis phase we see the employment of various on-scene and peri-scene psychological support interventions.

II. Individual crisis support can be applied on-scene during a crisis event or at anytime after such an event. The key factor here is that this intervention is done one-on-one, that is, one individual support person assisting one (or perhaps two) individual(s) in crisis.

III. "Demobilizations" are used at mass disaster venues to assist rescue and disaster response personnel to decompress and transition from the disaster site to home or work. Upon occasion, the demobilization will be used with primary victims.

The demobilization consists of a process wherein individuals, once disengaged from the crisis venue, receive refreshments and an informational briefing about stress, trauma, and coping techniques. It usually takes about 20 - 30 minutes.

IV. "Defusings" may be done at the crisis venue after disengagement from the crisis activity or in the post-crisis phase within 12 hours after a crisis. Defusings are 20 - 45 minute group discussions of the crisis event designed to reduce acute stress and tension levels.

V. "Critical Incident Stress Debriefings" (CISD) are also group discussions of a crisis or traumatic event. Their goal is to achieve a sense of psychological closure with regard to the crisis event. As a result, the CISD is usually most effective if done two to seven days after the crisis has concluded. They usually take one to three hours to complete.

VI. Any person who belongs to a family unit and experiences a crisis brings the effects of the crisis home to the other family members in both direct and indirect ways. Some form of post-incident family, or "significant other" support is highly encouraged. Religious / spiritual support is often provided within such services, but can obviously be applied wherever they are best received.

VII. One of the great values of critical incident stress management services is that they serve as a feeder system, or facilitator, for the utilization of more formal mental health assessment and treatment services. Without crisis support services such as these it is likely that many individuals, who need such follow-up care, would simply not seek it out.

These CISM interventions will be discussed in greater detail later in this manual.

The British Psychological Society (1990) has recommended that crisis intervention techniques be combined. We agree. Mitchell and Everly (1996) argue for an even more highly integrated combinatorial program to insure the potency of the intervention. Bordow and Porritt (1979) were presumably the first to actually demonstrate the dose-response potency of combined crisis intervention technologies, such as we see in CISM, in a well-controlled investigation. Flannery (in press) has more recently demonstrated the effectiveness of a crisis intervention program, following CISM principles, in a series of investigations.

The value of the CISM concepts has been so recognized that they have been recommended and / or implemented by organizations such as the Federal Bureau of Investigation; Federal Aviation Administration; Bureau of Alcohol, Tobacco and Firearms; Airline Pilots Association; the Royal Australian Navy; the U.S. Air Force; the U.S. Marines; National Institute of Occupational Safety and Health; U.S. Marshals' Service; and the U.S. Coast Guard, as well as, local fire services, hospitals, and law enforcement agencies too numerous to mention.

SUMMARY

In this chapter, we have traced the historical roots of crisis intervention. We have proposed that the history of this specialty within clinical mental health services is actually marked by two eras, or epochs.

Epoch One saw the advent of the notions of community outreach and preventive mental health services, as well as the use of paraprofessionals. Epoch Two saw the increasing sophistication with which the concepts of Epoch One were applied in the form of a multicomponent, integrated system of service provision which comprehensively spans the entire crisis spectrum from pre-crisis planning and on-scene support services, through referral for formal mental health assessment and treatment, if necessary.

Finally, we addressed the issue of establishing CISM as a standard of care in the provision of crisis intervention services, an idea which has gained significant empirical support (Everly, 1997).

CHAPTER TWO

The Risks of Psychological Crisis

Everyone will experience disturbances in their daily routines, lifestyles, and / or careers. Whether these disturbances are experienced as crises as we have earlier defined them is but a matter of the degree, or intensity, of their felt impact.

The perspective taken by this volume denotes a crisis as a significant inability to cope with a developmental or situational challenge such that one is left overwhelmed, confused, and defenseless against the challenge. Clinically speaking, a crisis is often equated with a traumatic event.

Just what are the risks of being exposed to psychological traumas? Consider this:

• The lifetime prevalence of trauma exposure in the U.S. has been estimated to be about 60% for males and 51% for females (Kessler, et al., 1995).

• The rate of trauma exposure for children and adolescents has been estimated to be about 40% (see Ford, Ruzek, and Niles, 1996).

• The lifetime prevalence of criminal victimization was assessed among female HMO patients and was found to be about 57% (Koss, et al., 1991).

- The U.S. Justice Department has determined that 1 in 6 violent crimes occur at the worksite (Bureau of Justice Statistics, Department of Justice, 1994).
- 14% of all homicides occur at the worksite.
- Homicide is the **third** leading cause of death from injury at the worksite (NIOSH) in the U.S., but in California and the District of Columbia it is the **leading** cause of workplace death (Cal-OSHA, 1994)!
- At the workplace, where the average person spends 1/3 of his / her life, there were over 1,000 murders and over 150,000 assaults, in 1994 (National Institute of Occupational Safety and Health, CIB 57).
- Violent crime at work costs over 1.75 million lost work days (Bureau of Justice Statistics, 1994).
- Law enforcement officers are 8.6 times more likely to die from suicide than from homicide and are 3.1 times more likely to die from suicide than from accidental circumstances (Violanti, 1996).
- 62% of the clinical healthcare staff sampled reported being exposed to a traumatic stressor at work (Caldwell, 1992).
- The prevalence of posttraumatic stress disorder ranged from 15% to 31% for samples of urban firefighters based on a traumatic exposure prevalence ranging from 85% to 91% (Beaton, Murphy, and Corneil, 1996).
- Symptoms of distress are correlated with exposure to traumatic stressors (Weiss, et al., 1988; Corneil, 1993).

So clearly, trauma and crisis is at epidemic proportions in the U.S.! It seems clear that such crisis events represent a "clear and present danger" to the psychological health of American society.

CRISIS-RELATED SYMPTOM PATTERNS

Earlier we defined crisis as a disequilibrium, that is, a disruption of the "steady state" of psychological processing that the mind fights to maintain. When faced with minor challenges or daily frustrations, the mind employs various compensatory mechanisms. Commonly used compensatory mechanisms might include denial of the problem, rationalization, intellectualization, creation of a psychological carapace, and / or problem solving techniques. Some of these compensation mechanisms are obviously more constructive in the long-term than are others. Nevertheless, they all work to quickly reestablish a psychological equilibrium in the face of a perturbation. Crises arise when the coping, or compensatory, mechanisms one usually employs prove ineffectual. Thus, the perceived challenge cannot be resolved to the satisfaction of the person experiencing the crisis. It is during such periods as these that symptoms of decompensation begin to manifest themselves. Decompensation results when the individual cannot cope with a crisis condition and therefore cannot reestablish psychological homeostasis.

Decompensation - a breakdown in psychological homeostasis evidenced by a potentially wide and diverse collection of psychological symptoms and maladaptive behavior patterns

---

The following represents a partial list of the most common crisis-related psychological and behavioral presentations, sometimes thought of as decompensation patterns or symptoms.

Panic

A panic attack is best thought of as a discrete paroxysmal interval of intense fear, psychological discomfort, and extreme psychophysiological arousal.

Psychological / behavioral symptoms of panic often include:

- the belief that one is dying
- extreme fear
- uncertainty
- hopelessness
- a sense of acute environmental constriction
- possible phobia formation

Physiological symptoms can be diverse and remarkably varied between individuals. They may include, but not be limited to:

- sweating
- cardiac palpitations
- tachycardia
- bradycardia
- nausea
- vertigo
- hyperventilation

Depression

It should be obvious that depression is not a single monolithic disorder, but rather represents a spectrum of symptom conditions. We are obviously most concerned with the more severe pole of the depression continuum.

The primary psychological symptoms of depression include:

- depressed mood
- anhedonia
- hopelessness
- helplessness
- suicidal ideation.

The classic physical symptoms of depression include:
- loss of appetite
- weight loss potential
- diminished libido
- terminal insomnia
- psychomotor retardation
- diminished energy.

Hypomania

While hypomania may appear similar to anxiety, it is different. Hypomania represents a discrete several day period characterized by irritable or elevated mood. More specifically, individuals may exhibit:
- a decreased need for sleep (2 - 3 hours of sleep)
- a rapid flow of ideas, rapid talkativeness
- inflated sense of self
- grandiosity, or perhaps even paranoid-like ideation.

Some hypomanic episodes may include extremely impulsive buying, gambling, or sexual behavior. Some individuals may attempt some form of self medication to compensate for this condition. Alcohol and other central nervous system depressants are commonly used.

Somatoform Conversion Reactions

The conversion variation of the somatoform disorder is typified by deficits in the motor and / or sensory systems. Psychological factors are the cause of, or major augmenting factor in, this array of physical dysfunctions which cannot be explained on the basis of pathophysiologic processes alone. Examples of conversion disorders would be:

- conversion blindness
- paralysis
- mutism
- deafness
- great difficulty swallowing

Historically these disorders were referred to as "hysterical" disorders.

Acute Stress Disorder (ASD)

This diagnostic category was first officially introduced in the diagnostic nosology of the American Psychiatric Association in 1994. It is considered an anxiety disorder which lasts for a minimum of two days and a maximum of four weeks. The initiation of the symptoms must occur within four weeks of a traumatic event. The symptoms may include symptoms such as:

- depersonalization, derealization, and numbing
- recollective ideation of the traumatic event such as dreams, flashbacks, or recurrent thoughts / images of the traumatic event
- avoidance of people, places, or things associated with the trauma
- symptoms of anxiety and autonomic nervous system hyperarousal.

Obviously the manifest symptom spectrum may vary markedly from person to person.

Posttraumatic Stress Disorder (PTSD)

This diagnostic category was first officially introduced in the Diagnostic and Statistical Manual of Mental Disorders, Third Edition (APA, 1980). The 1994 revision of that diagnostic taxonomy indicates that PTSD is a rather predictable sequelae of symptoms which lie in the wake of psychological trauma. Its key features include three symptom clusters subsequent to the exposure to a traumatic event:

> 1) recollection of the traumatic event in the form of persistent and distressing dreams, flashbacks, and / or intrusive thoughts / images;
>
> 2) persistent avoidance of people, places, and / or things associated with the traumatic event; and
>
> 3) persistent symptoms of increased arousal, such as hyperstartle reactions, irritability, angry outbursts, and sleep maintenance insomnia.

The diagnosis of PTSD does not overlap with ASD; therefore, the diagnosis cannot be made until the symptom duration has been at least one month. The delayed variant of PTSD is characterized by a symptom latency period of at least six months after the traumatic event.

Everly (Everly and Lating, 1995) has analyzed the posttraumatic stress disorder construct and found it to reveal two key components or constituents:

> 1) neurologic hypersensitivity and
>
> 2) psychologic hypersensitivity (Everly, 1993).

The neurologic hypersensitivity is thought to consist of a lowered depolarization threshold within the amygdala posterior hypothalamic efferent pathways of the limbic system, as well as other limbic-related structures such as the anterior pituitary. This functional hypersensitivity is thought to give rise to a potential over-reactive cascade of systemic hormonal phenomena, as well as behavioral impulsivity, irritability, and propensity for violence. The limbic hypersensitivity itself appears to result from:

> 1) an excess of excitatory neurotransmitters,
>
> 2) a paucity of inhibitory neurotransmitters, and / or

3) actual changes in dendritic receptor structures caused by chemical or genetic alterations (Everly, 1993).

The psychologic hypersensitivity is thought to arise from a violation of some deeply held belief. This belief is referred to as a worldview, or "Weltanschauung." Thus, a traumatic event, according to this perspective, is predicated upon some situation that violates a deeply-held and important worldview. Most commonly, we think of the traumatic event being a life threatening event - thus a violation to the assumption of safety discussed by writers such as Maslow (1970). Everly (1996) has identified four themes that seem universally traumatogenetic:

1) Violation of the belief that the world is "just" or "fair" Thus, why does an infant die in a motor vehicle accident?

2) Violation of a sense of who you are by having not done something you should, or by having done something you should not have done.

3) Abandonment, betrayal, violation of trust.

4) Violation of a sense of safety, universally speaking.

Grief / Bereavement Reactions

Grief and bereavement are normal reactions to loss. These reactions become pathognomonic when their intensity and / or chronicity become excessive that is, unusually debilitating to one's life. Many current formulations argue that grief and bereavement reactions are, by definition, pathognomonic when they satisfy the diagnostic criteria for a major depressive episode. Generally speaking, it may be suggested that normal grief reactions will not include extreme guilt reactions, feelings of worthlessness, or psychomotor retardation.

Psychophysiological Disorders

Psychophysiological disorders may be thought of as stress-related physiologic disorders related to crisis or trauma. Unlike the diagnosis of somatoform conversion reactions where there is no clear-cut pathophysiologic mechanism, the psychophysiologic disorder has a relatively well understood mechanism of pathophysiology. While the somatoform conversion reaction only affects the sensory or motor systems, the psychophysiologic disorder can affect any system in the human body (see Everly, 1989 for a review of the physiology of stress response mechanisms). Psychophysiologic disorders not only represent medical conditions caused by extreme stress, but include medical conditions exacerbated by extreme stress, as well.

Brief Reactive Psychosis

In rare instances a crisis or traumatic stressor may be of such intensity as to cause a brief psychotic episode. The symptoms of such a reaction would include either delusions, hallucinations, disorganized / incoherent speech, and / or disorganized, bizarre, or catatonic behavior. The duration of such a reactive episode is at least one day but is less than one month, according to the American Psychiatric Association's diagnostic nosology (APA, 1994).

Obsessive-Compulsive Disorders

A crisis, as noted early, engenders a process of decompensation. Some individuals, in an attempt to recompensate, demonstrate obsessive and / or compulsive symptom patterns. Such symptom patterns may include repetitive and persistent thoughts (obsessions) and / or repetitive behaviors or the unrealistically rigid adherence to rules, rituals, and routines (compulsions).

Other Crisis-related Symptoms

In addition to the aforementioned crisis-related symptom patterns, there exist several other significant maladaptive responses to crisis. Anger and violence appear to be on the rise as maladaptive responses to crisis. In their most extreme form these reactions may lead to homicidal ideation, gestures, and actual acts.

Lastly, we must mention suicide as a maladaptive coping mechanism to crisis. For many, suicide represents a "permanent solution" to what is often a temporary problem. And even then, the "solution" is not without a significant legacy of pain and problems for the friends and family members of the deceased.

SUMMARY

While clearly, there is a vast array of crisis related symptoms, we have enumerated some of the most common that the crisis interventionist is likely to encounter.

The brief summaries provided in this chapter are not intended to be formal diagnostic guidelines, but rather to be merely a guide to generating a working hypotheses during a crisis situation. Formal diagnosis is typically the domain of the clinician working outside of the crisis venue with the aid of the opportunity to conduct a clinical interview, complete mental status exam, psychiatric history, and psychological testing protocols.

CHAPTER THREE

Acute Crisis Assessment

The assessment of the risk and intensity of a psychological crisis is not an easy task. Formal risk and symptom assessments are obviously the exclusive domain of the mental health professions. Guidelines for conducting such formal assessments are far beyond the scope of this volume. Nevertheless, even the paraprofessional must have some sense of how to gage the risk and overall severity of manifest symptoms. This chapter shall offer some brief checklist - like suggestions, but not a substitute for assessment by a psychiatrist or psychologist.

ACUTE MENTAL STATUS ASSESSMENT

The form of assessment most suited for acute psychological crisis intervention is the acute mental status examination.

There are two types of mental status assessments: active and passive. The active mental status examination is where the crisis interventionist not only listens and observes the person in distress, but also actively challenges that person cognitively. Such active challenges include simple arithmetic calculations, such as, "Please add the following numbers and give me the total when I'm finished: 3, 7, 5, 2, and 1." Another type of challenge would be serial digit declarations, such as, "Please count backwards from 100 by 3s." Another type of challenge assesses specifically concentration and short-term memory. For example, "Please repeat this phrase after me: John Smith lives at 98 East Maple Street, Baltimore, Maryland." Then two to three minutes later, the person is asked to recall that phrase. These are but a few examples of active mental exam assessment processes. They are usually not indicated for acute crisis situations.

The passive mental status exam is more useful in crisis and is based upon conversational assessment and observation. The passive exam, when done well, is difficult to distinguish from merely concerned conversational discourse.

Because it is based upon inference, the passive exam must be sensitive to recognizing:

1) unusual behavior,

2) bizarre behavior,

3) potentially injurious behavior (to self or others),

4) any evidence of psychotic process, or

5) any behavior that would suggest that the person is functionally impaired.

A TWO-STAGE PROCESS

Whether one uses an active or passive assessment paradigm one should have a basic assessment structure in mind. A simple two-stage structure is usually pragmatic but often revealing.

Stage One: Rule Out:

1) Medical instability, if possible; for example, evidence of serious bleeding or difficulty breathing.

2) Closed head injury leaving the person partially conscious or partially responsive.

3) Intoxication
   a. Alcohol
   b. Stimulants (e.g., cocaine, ampletamine, caffeine)
   c. Illicit depressants
   d. Antihistamines
   e. Hallucinogenic substances
4) Psychotic Process
   a. Hallucinations
   b. Delusions
5) Injurious Potential (these will be addressed in more detail later in this chapter)
   a. Violent or homicidal inclinations
   b. Suicidal inclinations

Any of these factors, if present, or if unable to be ruled as nonexisting, serve to contradict the assumption that the person in distress is capable of independent functioning. As a result, some form of protective and remedial action will be necessary. While they will vary from situation to situation resources such as family members, clergy, the police, the local emergency room, the company physician, psychologist, or EAP may all be potential options depending upon the severity of the situation.

Stage Two: Cognitive Affective Assessment
   1) Cognition is often assessed in four domains:
      a. Orientation (person, place, time)
      b. Concentration
      c. Short-term memory
      d. Long-term memory
   2) Affect, or emotion, is generally assessed with regard to:
      a. situational appropriateness and

b. intensity (functional or dysfunctional)

Obviously any extreme or disabling disturbance of cognition or emotion will require escalation of the intervention as noted above and follow-up.

In the next two sections, we shall look at the assessment of violence and suicidal risk in more detail.

VIOLENCE

Contrary to popular belief, violent behavior is very difficult to predict. So difficult, in fact, that both the American Psychological Association and the American Psychiatric Association have declared that their professionals are unable to reliably do so. Nevertheless, Ziegler (1992) has reviewed the relevant literature and offers some general factors which seem to increase the risk of violence. They are simply listed below:

1) Past history of violence toward animals or humans.

2) Presence of a psychiatric disorder.

3) Expressed intention to commit harm to self or others.

4) Bizarre behavior or intention expressed.

5) Recent personal loss experienced.

6) Age range 15 - 34 years represents highest risk. Males represent three times the risk of suicide compared to females.

7) Previous attempts at suicide or violence towards others.

8) Refusal of assistance or care when offered.

9) Command hallucinations.

SUICIDE

Any of Ziegler's (1992) criteria, when present, increase the risk of suicidal and homicidal behavior. He emphasizes how suicide and homicide interrelate.

Historically, the following factors have been believed to increase the risk of suicide specifically:

1) Previous suicide attempts

2) History of suicide in the family

3) Isolation

4) Close proximity to, or availability of, lethal means
    (e.g., drugs, guns, etc.)

5) Psychiatric history

6) Financial or marital problems

7) Painful or terminal illness

8) Severe guilt or depression

9) Hopelessness or helplessness

10) Evidence of a premeditated plan.

Both the violent and the suicidal individual are usually plagued by a sense of being out of control, feeling overwhelmed, feeling hopeless, or helpless.

A useful "rule of thumb" when confronted with these individuals is to attempt to empower the person in crisis, that is, attempt to contradict their sense of hopelessness. This must be achieved, however, without putting oneself at greater risk and without disregarding his or her suffering.

SUMMARY

This chapter was designed to simply provide a brief checklist - like introduction to crisis assessment highlighting common issues of relevance during an acute decompensation process. It was not designed to be comprehensive nor a stand alone guide to crisis or mental status assessment. An excellent guide to mental status assessment is that of Stub and Black (1993).

In an earlier chapter, we noted that crisis intervention, generically, was designed to reduce distress and assist in the restoration of independent functioning (i.e., psychological and behavioral homeostasis). It seems rational that crisis intervention techniques will not always achieve this end, no matter how skillfully they are implemented. As a result, more formal and focused psychological assessment and / or therapeutic intervention will be required. It seems reasonable that the presence of various conditions would mandate follow-up assessment and / or care:

1) Disabling symptoms of the crisis
2) Persistent symptoms of the crisis (lasting more than about a week)
3) Any evidence of cognitive impairment
4) Any evidence of suicidal, homicidal, or violent intention
5) Whenever in doubt

The actual targets for referral could include, but not be limited to:

1) Medical services
2) Psychological services
3) Psychiatric services
4) Religious or spiritual services
5) Family support services
6) Financial aid services
7) Career counseling
8) Legal services

In some instances several of these services will need to be combined to best serve the person in distress.

CHAPTER FOUR

Basic Communication Techniques In Crisis: The Foundation Of Critical Incident Stress Management

It is the aim of this volume to introduce the reader to the principles and components of critical incident stress management (CISM), a new generation in the delivery of crisis intervention services. As noted earlier CISM represents an integrated multicomponent crisis intervention system. The core technologies within the CISM framework will be reviewed later in this text; however, it is the purpose of this chapter to lay the foundation upon which all CISM technologies are ultimately based - basic communication processes.

BASIC COMMUNICATION TECHNIQUES

These are several communication techniques that may prove especially useful in crisis situations.

Silence - It may seem contradictory to begin a section on communication techniques with silence; however, silence can be a powerful tool in a crisis situation. Silence can be effectively used to avoid intrusion and facilitate uninterrupted catharsis. Silence can also be used as a means of showing support as well as respect for the person in crisis. Silence becomes counterproductive if used excessively and conveys confusion or a lack of interest.

<u>Nonverbal Attending</u> - refers to the process of attending to and monitoring the nonverbal behavior, also known as "body language" exhibited by the person in crisis. There are no hard and fast rules pertaining to just what certain postures or gestures actually mean. Rather, the crisis interventionist should monitor for obvious changes and whether these changes facilitate or inhibit communication.

<u>Restatement</u> - is where the interventionist literally restates a key phrase or important point that has been made by the person in crisis. In this technique, the interventionist uses the <u>same</u> key words as did the person in crisis. This technique is used to check for listening accuracy and to clarify semantically ambiguous terms.

<u>Paraphrasing</u> - is the term used to denote when the support person uses his / her own words to summarize the main points or theme of what the person in crisis has just said. This technique is more conversational than it is restatement. It can be used to check for listening accuracy, to clarify ambiguities, to allow the speaker to "hear" what he / she has just said, or simply to probe for further clarification / elaboration. For example, one might begin the paraphrase by saying, "So, in other words . . . ."

<u>Reflection of Emotion</u> - refers to the technique by which the support person "mirrors," or reflects back to the person in crisis the nature of the emotions that have just been observed. For example, "You look like you're angry." This technique is useful for helping individuals talk about emotions that they might be otherwise hesitant to disclose. It also acknowledges the presence of emotions and accepts those emotions within the crisis situation.

Open-end Questions - These are questions that tend not to restrict the response options available to the person being asked the question. Open-end questions typically begin with words such as:

> "What"
> "How"
> "Why"
> "Describe," or
> "Tell me . . ."

Use of the open-end question can foster introspection. Excessive use can overwhelm someone in crisis.

Closed-end Questions - These questions are structured so as to restrict, focus, or direct the responses of the respondent. Closed-end questions typically begin with:

"Is"	"Do"	"When"
"Where"	"Can"	"Who"
"Did"	"Would"	"Could"
"Should"	"Shall"	"Have"
"Are"	"Where"	"Which"

The most closed-end question of all questions is, of course, the question that must be answered with a "yes" or "no" response. A long series of "yes - no" questions can be frustrating to the respondent and restrictive even for the crisis interventionist.

QUESTION PATTERNS

The most effective use of questions is one which combines both open-end and closed-end questions in the most productive manner. In some situations, it will be most productive to begin with a closed-end question to establish a point or fact and then follow with and open-end question to gain elaboration. For example:

> **Closed-end question:** "Have you ever been in a crisis like this before?"
>
> **Response:** "Yes."
>
> **Open-end question:** "What was that like?"

This structure is often referred to as the ***inverted funnel technique.***

In some situations it will be most productive to begin with an open-end question and then follow with a closed-end question to focus or better direct the next response. For example:

> **Open-end question:** "What happened?"
>
> **Response:** "I've been having problems at work and problems at home."
>
> **Closed-end question:** "Which is most distressing to you right now?"
>
> **Response:** "I guess my problems at home are most troublesome to me now."

This structure is called a ***funnel technique***. A logical follow-up to this series would be to use another open-end question such as:

> **Open-end question:** "So, what do your problems at home consist of?"

Effective technique selection certainly improves with experience. **Nevertheless, the most important aspect of effective crisis communication is *listening*.** Through listening the crisis interventionist is able to assess both the nature of the crisis situation as well as the psychological status of the person in crisis.

Table 4.1 reviews the basic communication techniques.

AN ACUTE EMOTIONAL DE-ESCALATION TECHNIQUE

Crises are often fraught with acute emotional turmoil. Such turmoil can often feed upon itself and create a self-fueling affective spiral which can serve as a major block to crisis response. Thus

TABLE 4.1
BASIC COMMUNICATION TECHNIQUES

TECHNIQUE	PURPOSE	COMMENT
SILENCE	• to promote speech • to encourage continued uninterrupted speech	Careful! May inadvertently communicate noncaring, lack of interest.
NON VERBAL ATTENDING	• to encourage continued uninterrupted speech • to probe • to show interest	Nodding of the head and facial expressions are examples.
RESTATEMENT	• to show you are listening • to check for accuracy • to clarify semantics • to probe	Careful! Used too frequently, you can sound like a mindless parrot. Good to clarify semantic ambiguities.
PARAPHRASING	• to communicate interest, understanding, empathy • to check for listening accuracy to allow speaker to "hear" own thoughts • to probe for further content	Use more frequently than restatement. Easier and more natural than restatement. A powerful behavior change technique.
REFLECTION OF EMOTION	• to identify the speaker's feelings based on verbal and/or nonverbal cues • to encourage discussion of feelings and remove emotional blocks to communication	Important to allow feelings to be expressed, otherwise they block problem solving and tend to escalate. But be careful! Don't overuse this technique.
OPEN-END QUESTIONS	• to provide maximal response options • to question without restricting answers	Good to use in early phases. Use when you get "stuck."
CLOSED-END QUESTIONS	• to direct or focus responses • to provide structure	Good when pursuing a specific target. You only learn what you know to ask.

when a crisis interventionist encounters emotional discord which seems to be escalating or self-sustaining it is important to attempt to stabilize the emotional environment. There are several steps that one can follow that may be of value as one tries to manage emotionally charged situations.

Initially, it is important to listen for several moments, if possible, in order to ascertain the reason for the emotional discharge. Whether this is practical will depend on the specifics of the situation. If practical, determine the type of emotion.

The first overtly active intervention becomes verbally identifying the emotions being expressed. The crisis communication technique best suited for this purpose is the "reflection of emotions." An example would be, "You seem really angry right now." If identification of the specific emotion is difficult, simply use a more generic approach, such as, "You seem really upset right now." It is important to attempt to engage the person in distress in some form of structured dialogue.

A typical follow-up to this reflection of emotions is to inquire as to the specific nature of the crisis. An inquiry such as, "What is causing you to be so upset?" often helps identify the source of the crisis. Or one might simply say, "What's going on?"

Once some indication of the source of the crisis is provided, the use of the communication technique of "paraphrasing" becomes valuable. This technique is designed to interrupt the tirade as well as show interest, concern, and to check for the accuracy of one's interpretation of the situation.

Ideally, at this point, the self-fueling emotional spiral has been interrupted. The task of acute emotional de-escalation has been achieved. Typically, the crisis intervention process shifts to stabilization and crisis resolution. Table 4.2 summarizes this technique.

TABLE 4.2

ACUTE DE-ESCALATION TECHNIQUES

STEP 1: Reflection of emotions -
"You seem to be feeling . . ."

STEP 2: Open-end question -
" What's making you feel that way?"

STEP 3: Paraphrase -
"So, in other words . . ."

CHANGING BEHAVIOR

In a crisis situation, it is often the intention of the interventionist to change the acute behavior of the person in crisis. Demanding directives, threats, or coercion seldom prove effective. If they do prove effective acutely, they tend to engender feelings of resentment subsequent to the acute crisis situation. Change, even acute change, comes from within the person demonstrating the change. A person changes because the change is perceived as a good idea at that moment. Thus, it is usually a good crisis intervention strategy to assist the person in crisis to see that a change in behavior is desirable (i.e., in his / her best interest). The paraphrase and the question can be subtle, yet powerful tools to facilitate change.

A person who is in crisis often feels out of control, powerless, and sometimes even helpless. To immediately tell the person in crisis what to do, (i.e., what is best) may be perceived as infantilizing or may even add to the sense of powerlessness. An important exception to this principle is when the person in crisis is feeling so overwhelmed that direct advice is perceived as being very welcomed and even sought after. Thus to avoid the risk of engendering resentment, infantilization, or even reactions that are just the opposite of what one may ask or demand the person in crisis to do, the behavior change strategy of paraphrasing and asking introspective questions may prove of value.

The use of paraphrasing techniques may seem inefficient, but it should be remembered that in most crises the passage of time serves as a natural de-escalation technique. Hostage negotiators employ just this principle. An exception to this rule is when anyone associated with this crisis situation is medically unstable.

How can paraphrasing techniques and questions that cause the person to engage in introspection prove of value in the crisis situation? Paraphrases and questions typically cause the individual to examine and analyze his / her behavior. These techniques, then, serve as a form of psychological mirror causing one to scrutinize one's actions, and gives the interventionist the opportunity to point out the ramifications of one's actions that may not have been considered. Often times, upon reanalysis and considering the results of his / her actions, the person is able to discover more constructive crisis coping techniques.

Example #1:

> **Crisis statement:** " I hate this job so much I just want to quit. I've got 10 years invested in it, but I just feel like quitting."

> **Paraphrase and Question:** "So in other words you dislike the job so much you're willing to give up your seniority and pension to get out? Do you think that is really the best option for you?"

Example #2:

> **Crisis statement:** "Life is hopeless, nothing I do turns out right. The only thing I can do is kill myself."

> **Paraphrase and Question:** "Sounds like you're feeling

so out of control of your life that suicide seems like a viable solution. Is that really the only way for you to get back a sense of control?"

The other advantage to the use of those techniques, as noted earlier, is that they facilitate the passage of time. This, in and of itself, tends to often reduce the lability of the emotions of the person in crisis.

Finally, paraphrases and nonthreatening questions can be used to transition from affective expression to a more cognitive processing of the crisis. Such a shift is more likely to yield a resolution to the crisis situation.

SUMMARY

In this chapter we had attempted to provide a functional overview of the foundation of all CISM interventions - communication techniques. Rather than be exhaustive in our review, we have chosen to simply review those techniques and processes that have the greatest potential for utility in acute crisis situations. As one develops expertise in the use of these communication techniques, one increases the ability to "think on your feet" and function innovatively in a wide variety of diverse crisis situations. Mastery of these techniques yields pragmatic flexibility - a key to successful crisis response.

CHAPTER FIVE

The CISM Interventions

In the previous chapter, it was argued that basic communication lies at the foundation of effective crisis response. In effect, all crisis response interventions are ultimately based upon effective communications. The purpose of this current chapter is to familiarize the reader with specific CISM interventions. Close observation reveals that no matter what the protocol, it will be grounded in the dynamics of human communications. Although grounded in good communication protocols, there is also value in having a psychological roadmap, of sorts, to follow as one is engaged in a crisis response. Clinically, we refer to protocols, or clinical pathways, that give a sense of order and direction to our efforts at intervention.

In this chapter, the seven core CISM interventions are functionally reviewed. This chapter is not designed to do anything other than provide an overview. Mitchell and Everly (1996) have constructed a detailed operations manual for those interested in actually implementing these protocols.

To review, briefly, the core seven CISM interventions are:

1) Pre-incident preparedness training
2) One-on-one individual psychological support
   (1 to 3 sessions)
3) Demobilizations

4) Critical Incident Stress Debriefing (CISD)

5) Defusing

6) Family support

7) Referral mechanisms

The collective goals of these CISM interventions within the crisis response clinical genre are:

1) To reduce the incidence, duration, and severity of, or impairment from, traumatic stress arising from crisis and disaster situations and

2) To facilitate access to formal mental health assessment and treatment, if needed.

Thus, these interventions are consistent with Caplan's (1964) conceptualization of primary, secondary, and tertiary prevention paradigms.

Let's take a closer look at the core CISM interventions:

PRE-INCIDENT PREPARATION:
PSYCHOLOGICAL PREPAREDNESS TRAINING

Definition: Psychological preparedness training is consistent with Caplan's (1964) notion of a primary prevention technology. Implemented prior to the actual crisis event, this intervention is designed to set the appropriate expectation for the crisis / disaster experience while enhancing the behavioral response to crisis. This intervention has also been referred to as "pre-incident education" or "mental preparedness training."

Uses: Psychological preparedness training may be instituted:

> 1) in a formal training venue for high risk personnel (such as a training academy or training institute) prior to any job or career wherein one may encounter a significant crisis; and / or
>
> 2) for emergency response and disaster personnel prior to deployment at each different disaster venue.

Goals: The goals of the psychological preparedness intervention include (Everly, 1995b):

> 1) setting appropriate expectations for actual experiences,
>
> 2) increasing cognitive resources relevant to a crisis, and
>
> 3) teaching behavioral stress management and personal coping techniques, all with the specific goal of preventing psychological dysfunction and disorder (Weisaeth, 1989; Hytten and Hasle, 1989; Solomon and Benbenishty, 1986).

Format: According to Everly (1995), the psychological preparedness training intervention should possess three components delivered, ideally, within a group format.

First, "information" should be communicated regarding the nature of stress, and the nature of psychological trauma.

Second, specific "expectations" should be set as to:

1) the nature of the most common types of crises and stressors faced and

2) the nature of the most common signs and symptoms of psychological discord.

Thirdly, specific behavioral stress management and personal "coping" techniques should be taught and rehearsed so as to improve functioning during *and* after a crisis.

ONE-ON-ONE INDIVIDUAL CRISIS SUPPORT:
THE SAFER MODEL

Definition: Effective crisis response is more than just thinking on your feet or being glib. Effective crisis response is predicated upon knowledge and skill. While no two crises will be exactly the same, research and empirical observation have taught us that it is usually helpful to follow somewhat of a course, "psychological roadmap," or protocol during the process of one's crisis response intervention. The use of well-honed protocols will be emphasized in our discussions of Critical Incident Stress Debriefing and defusing. Both are group crisis response interventions. But what of intervening with a single individual who is in crisis? In actuality, most crisis response interventions will be done individually, that is, one-on-one, rather than in groups.

The SAFER model represents a protocol for conducting individual crisis response interventions. As such, it may be a useful psychological roadmap to follow as one assists an individual in crisis.

Uses: The SAFER model is designed for use with individuals in crisis, unlike the defusings as CISD models which are to be used with groups. The SAFER model may be used on-scene during an acute crisis or disaster situation, or anywhere and at anytime after the initial crisis impact.

Goals: The goals of the SAFER model are those of most acute crisis response protocols (i.e., to mitigate the acute distress of the individual in crisis and to facilitate access to follow-up mental health assessment and treatment, if needed.

Format: The SAFER model follows a specific progression. That progression is described in Table 5.1 and discussed in some detail subsequently.

TABLE 5.1
A Summary of the SAFER Model

STAGE	CONTENT	ACTION	GOAL
ONE	Stabilization of the Situation	To remove the person in crisis from provocative stressors.	To mitigate affective escalation. Allows mental status assessment.
TWO	Acknowledgment of Crisis	To have person in crisis describe "what happened" and personal reactions to the crisis.	To encourage cathartic ventilation to reduce arousal; establish rapport and a sense of safety.
THREE	Facilitation of Understanding	To explain symptoms. To view symptoms in context of survival mechanisms.	To have the person in crisis view symptoms as "normal" reactions albeit potentially problematic.
FOUR	Encouragement of Adaptive Coping	To teach basic stress / crisis management.	To improve immediate and short-term coping. To develop a plan for immediate use.
FIVE	Restoration of independent functioning, or referral for continued care	Assessment of current adaptive functioning as adequate or seek further assistance.	Reestablishment of psychological homeostasis or provision of continued acute care.

Stabilization of the Situation

In this initial step in the SAFER protocol, the crisis interventionist assesses the impact that the immediate environment is having on the person in crisis and acts to remove the person from any provocative stressors (people or things) that may be sustaining the crisis. This can be achieved by "taking a walk," "getting a cup of coffee," or any other diversionary process that provides the individual with some "psychological distance" away from the source of the acute crisis or any other cues that appear to fuel the crisis situation. Prior to any such intervention, however, the crisis interventionist must always introduce him / herself and the role that is being served or performed.

Acknowledgment of the Crisis

The second step in the SAFER intervention is the acknowledgment of the crisis itself. This stage is fostered by a skillful use of basic helping communication techniques. In this stage, the crisis interventionist most typically asks the person to describe "what happened" to create the crisis situation. As a crisis is often punctuated by escalating emotions, this question gives the person in a crisis a cue and reason to return to the cognitive thinking domain, at least temporarily. Yet it is not usually advised to completely discourage cathartic ventilation, therefore, after having described the nature of the crisis situation, the person in crisis is asked to describe his / her current state of psychological functioning. A simple prompt such as, "How are you doing now?" allows the person who is in crisis to return to cathartic ventilation but now in a somewhat more structured and secure manner. Thus, we see within this stage, the crisis interventionist has superimposed cognitive oriented communications over the potentially labile emotional foundation. Later, however, having listened to the nature of the crisis, the interventionist encourages emotional ventilation in a safer, more structured communication environment.

Facilitation of Understanding

The third stage in the present model involves a transition back to the cognitive psychological domain for the person in crisis. In this third stage, the crisis interventionist begins to *actively* respond to the information revealed by the person in crisis during the previous stage. Here the person in crisis is encouraged to view his / her reactions to the crisis as generally "normal," expected reactions being experienced by a "normal" individual, in response to an abnormally challenging situation (i.e., a crisis situation). The primary goals of this stage of the SAFER model are:

> 1) to assist the person in crisis in returning to the cognitive domain of psychological processing and
>
> 2) to encourage the person in crisis to see his / her symptoms as basically "normal" reactions to an extraordinarily stressful event.

Encourage Adaptive Coping

The fourth stage of the model represents what is usually the most overtly active stage with regard to the behavior of the crisis interventionist. Here the interventionist engages in the teaching of basic concepts in 1) crisis and 2) stress and stress management. As with the previous stage, it takes place within the cognitive domain of psychological processing. Basic stress management techniques may be discussed and a *plan* for coping with the acute crisis situation is conjointly developed by the crisis interventionist and the person in crisis.

Restoration Of Independent Functioning Or Referral

The goal of the previous four stages is always to assist the person in reestablishing independent psychological and behavioral functioning. In the vast majority of cases, this will have been achieved by this point in the process. In some instances, however, it will be evident that the person in crisis is remaining in a highly unstable condition. If such is the case, the crisis interventionist's goal becomes that of providing assistance in obtaining continued acute care. Resources for such continued care might be family members, other departmental resources, or in extreme cases where no other resources seem suitable, an emergency room at a local hospital, or even law enforcement authorities.

To review, the SAFER model is designed for use by either peer counselors or by mental health trained professionals working with personnel who are in crisis. The model was five basic stages including a final resolution determination stage. The model includes several key elements within each stage:

        1) a content structure,

        2) a process domain,

        3) an action, and

        4) a goal.

These were presented in Table 5.1 earlier in this chapter.

DEMOBILIZATIONS

Definition: A demobilization is a group intervention technology. It is best conceived of as a transitional intervention which allows for psychological and psychophysiological decompression following disengagement from a large-scale crisis venue (Mitchell and Everly, 1996). This intervention may be used with primary victim populations as well as emergency response and rescue personnel.

Uses: The demobilization is used after large-scale crises, mass disasters, or crisis situations that have necessitated the mobilization and deployment of a large number of emergency responders (typically greater than 10). The demobilization can also be used with a large number of primary victims subsequent to a crisis / disaster.

Goals: The demobilization may be summarized as follows:

    1) To provide a psychological and temporal transition from the crisis event to some form of normalization;

    2) To provide an opportunity for psychological and psychophysiological decompression;

    3) To set realistic expectations for the psychological consequences of the crisis event;

    4) To provide education as to practical stress management techniques that may be employed; and,

    5) To facilitate access to other psychological and / or physical support systems.

Format: The demobilization requires a structured demobilization area where potentially large numbers of field personnel can go for the purpose of decompression, as noted above.

The venue for the demobilization is directly behind the working, or operational, lines of the disaster site, or at least in the immediate vicinity.

Operationally there are usually two segments employed in the demobilization:

1) the provision of food and rest (10 - 20 minutes) and
2) the provision of information on traumatic stress (especially signs and symptoms), stress management techniques, and follow-up options for further psychological and / or physical support (10 - 15 minutes).

The distribution of written handout material is extremely helpful. The utilization of verbal communications without written handouts as a backup may prove unreliable immediately after individuals leave the crisis venue.

CRITICAL INCIDENT STRESS DEBRIEFING (CISD)

Definition: The term Critical Incident Stress Debriefing (CISD) is actually a proper noun. It refers to the specific model of psychological debriefing developed by Dr. Jeffrey T. Mitchell in the United States (Mitchell, 1983; Mitchell and Everly, 1996) during the late 1970s and early 1980s.

There are certainly other models of psychological debriefing (a point of significant confusion for those who believe CISD is a generic term). For example, the American Red Cross uses a model adapted from Mitchell (Armstrong, O'Callahan, and Marmar, 1991), and Dunning (1988) developed an educational debriefing model. Nevertheless, Mitchell's CISD model of psychological debriefing is generally recognized as the most widely used in the world and is used across the greatest diversity of settings and operational applications.

Although originally developed for, and extensively used with, emergency response, rescue, and disaster management personnel, Mitchell's CISD has also been used in hospitals (Flannery, et al., 1995), banks (Leeman - Conley, 1990), courtrooms (Feldman and Bell, 1991), schools (Blackwelder, 1994; Dyregrov, 1990), the military (U.S. Air Force, 1995), and various business and industrial settings (for example, the airline industry and many employee assistance programs serving numerous and diverse organizations).

Uses: The CISD is utilized with a **homogenous** group of individuals who have experienced a crisis or traumatic event. Both primary victims, as well as secondary observers, such as emergency responders can utilize the CISD.

The technique should be used at least 24 hours after the traumatic event has ended; or at least 24 hours after individuals have been operationally disengaged from the event with no expectation of returning to the event, if it was on going.

Goals: Clearly the goal of the CISD is consistent with Caplan's (1964) formulation of the notion of secondary prevention. Thus CISD is designed to mitigate the adverse psychological impact of a traumatic event by reducing the intensity and chronicity of symptoms subsequent to the trauma. But most importantly, the goal of the CISD, which differentiates it from the defusing, is that the CISD is designed to bring or facilitate psychological *closure* to a traumatic event. As a result, the CISD is not designed to be repeated serially as might be the case with the defusing. Similarly, the CISD will not be used during an on-going disaster or traumatic event.

Format: The CISD consists of a 7 stage protocol described in Table 5.2.

	Table 5.2		
	The CISD Process		
CISD Phase	CISD Objectives	Leader's Prompts	Domain
Introduction	To introduce intervention team members, explain the process, and set expectations and ground rules.	"My name is... Our purpose for being here is ... The 'ground rules' are as follows..."	Cognitive
Fact	To allow participants to describe the traumatic event from his / her own perspective (ask each participant, but make it clear that one can choose to be silent).	"Tell me who you are, what your role in the incident was, and just what you saw and / or heard take place."	Cognitive
Thought	To allow participants to describe their cognitive reactions to the event and to begin to transition to the affective domain (once again ask each participant to volunteer his / her perspective).	"Now, I'd like you to tell us what your first thoughts were in response to the crisis."	Cognitive to Affective
Reaction	To identify the most traumatic aspect of the crisis for participants who wish to speak and to allow for cathartic ventilation (simply ask the probing question to the group, collectively).	"What was the worst part of the incident for you personally?"	Affective

	Table 5.2 cont'd.		
	The CISD Process		
CISD Phase	CISD Objectives	Leader's Prompts	Domain
Symptom	To identify any symptoms of distress or psychological discord that the group of participants wish to share and to potentiate the initial transition from the affective domain back to the cognitive domain.	"What physical or psychological symptoms have you noticed, if any, as a result of this incident?"	Affective to Cognitive
Teaching	To facilitate a return to the cognitive domain by normalizing and demedicalizing the crisis reactions of the participants and to teach the basic personal stress management / coping techniques that can be used to reduce current distress.	"We've heard numerous symptoms that are being experienced, let me explain their nature and give you some suggestions on how to reduce their negative impact."	Cognitive
Re-Entry	To provide closure to the CISD process, remembering that the goal of the CISD is to provide psychological closure to the crisis incident; answer any questions, and assess the need for follow-up actions / referrals.	"Let me try to summarize what we've covered during this process together."	Cognitive

DEFUSING

Definition: A small group discussion of a crisis or traumatic event.
Uses: The defusing is a group discussion which is more flexible than the CISD. It can easily be repeated according to the need (e.g., for shifts of rescue workers after a mass disaster). Ideally it is used within 12 hours of the crisis.

Goals: Like the CISD, the defusing is designed to reduce psychological tension and discord. Unlike the CISD, the defusing is not necessarily designed to achieve closure on a crisis, although it may. Basically, the defusing is designed to facilitate a restoration of functioning.

Format: The defusing has three phases:

Introduction - to introduce the intervention team, to explain the reason and goals of the intervention, and to cover the "ground rules," while setting expectations.

Exploration - to literally explore the nature and impact of the crisis. Two subphases are typically employed: Asking about the *facts* of the crisis and asking about personal *reactions* to the crisis.

Information - to teach basic concepts of stress and stress management while attempting to normalize symptoms and teach practical coping for this particular crisis.

FAMILY SUPPORT

Any given crisis can be contagious!

Any person who is part of a family unit and who has been affected by a crisis, trauma, or disaster brings the crisis home to the members of the family. The crisis can spread directly to family members through abuse, abandonment, violence, or neglect. The crisis can spread indirectly through isolation and withdrawal, occupational turmoil and jeopardy, self-medication, and the like.

Family support services should be part of any truly integrated CISM program. It may take more time and effort to establish such a program, but its absence clearly weakens the potential CISM effectiveness. Many military CISM programs are actually housed in family services.

Chaplain, or other religious-oriented crisis response elements, including pastoral counseling may be housed within the family support component of the CISM program because of their universal value to primary, secondary, or tertiary victims of crisis who are desirous of such intervention. Such religious-centered programs may be an aspect of other CISM elements as mentioned in the next section, as well.

REFERRAL MECHANISMS

One of the great values of an organized systematic intervention such as CISM is that it provides a unique opportunity to do field assessments and triaging. In effect, the opportunity to bring everyone involved in a critical incident together for a brief contact is afforded to the crisis response team.

Traditional formulations would require the individuals to seek out psychological support. Mitchell (1983) recognized there was significant resistance among certain groups to do that because of fears of looking "weak" or otherwise incompetent. This was evident in emergency medical services, the military, law enforcement, fire suppression, and airline industry and related fields. Yet these personnel were those at highest risk for PTSD and therefore, in greatest need of crisis support.

A standardized CISM program as part of a standing crisis plan insures everyone in the crisis will receive the opportunity for support. CISM programs don't compete with traditional mental health services. If implemented correctly CISM programs will enhance and compliment the delivery of traditional employee assistance and traditional mental health services.

Chapter Three addressed many of the symptoms that prompt referrals as well as the various targets for the referrals. To reiterate, referrals may be made for:

1) Psychological and / or psychiatric services,
2) Medical services,
3) Religious, spiritual services,
4) Family support services,
5) Financial aid services,
6) Career counseling, and
7) Legal services.

MANDATORY OR VOLUNTARY CISM SERVICES

The issue of whether CISM services should be mandatory or voluntary is an intriguing one. Solely voluntary services run the risk of underutilization based upon the stigma of needing help. Mandatory services raise issues of coercion, legal liability, and informed consent.

The Federal Aviation Administration has an interesting model worthy of consideration. Following a critical incident a mandatory, general information session is held for all those involved in the critical incident. Afterwards, a voluntary CISM intervention such as a defusing or CISD, is held. Participation rates are reportedly in excess of 95% for the voluntary components.

SUMMARY

In this chapter, we have reviewed the core seven CISM components. Ideally CISM is a multicomponent, integrated crisis response system. The elements appear to be synergistic, not just additive, and are designed to span the entire crisis spectrum from pre-crisis through post-crisis and follow-up. No one CISM intervention was ever meant to be a stand alone technique. This is especially true of the CISD.

No matter what the CISM intervention, it may be helpful to keep a few guidelines in mind.

1) CISM is a support function. Don't interfere with operational activities.

2) Don't intervene so as to jeopardize the ego defense mechanisms of the person in crisis.

3) Don't become overly analytical.

4) Don't confront or use "reverse psychology."

5) Don't moralize or "preach" to the person in crisis.

6) Don't progress too quickly within any CISM protocol. Remember as long as the person is medically stable, time is usually on your side.

7) Don't dismiss discussions of suicide, homicide or other acts of violence as merely verbal gestures, posturing, or manipulations. Failure to take even a veiled threat seriously could lead to escalations.

8) Don't take personal risks with your own well-being.

CHAPTER SIX

Mechanisms of Action in CISM

The term "mechanisms of action" refers to the mechanisms, or processes, through which any given intervention exerts its effect.

The notion of mechanisms of action, in essence, then refers to the processes which cause the intervention to be effective. In the study of psychopharmacology, for example, an understanding of the mechanisms of psychoactive drugs are considered essential to the viability and utilization of the drug. Drugs are sometimes prescribed for their "side effects" as well as their "main effects." But in general the use of any drug is made more effective by understanding, not just *if* it works, but *why* it works. The drug class known as selective serotonergic reuptake inhibitors, for example, derive their effectiveness from their ability to block the natural reuptake of the neurotransmitter serotinin at the presynaptic membranes. The mechanisms of action for psychological and behavioral interventions are usually more subtle and less well understood. Nevertheless, any intervention that exerts any effect at all must, by definition, have some mechanism of action that accounts for that effect. Psychological interventions most likely have many complex interacting mechanisms at the root of their effectiveness. While more complicated in terms of processes, the necessity to understand the mechanisms of action undergirding psychological and behavioral interventions is no less important.

The study of putative mechanisms of action is an important one if we are to improve our interventions and continue to innovate. Such scrutiny teaches us why our interventions succeed and why they fail; they allow us to "troubleshoot" complicated situations, as well.

The previous chapter provided a working overview of the interventions which comprise the critical incident stress management (CISM) crisis response system. The next logical step in understanding the CISM system is an analysis of the mechanisms upon which CISM is built.

In this chapter, we shall review and speculate upon the mechanisms of action which undergird CISM. We shall begin with an analysis of crisis intervention as a genre then move to more specific analyses.

CRISIS INTERVENTION VERSUS PSYCHOTHERAPY

The practice of the art of crisis intervention is very different than the practice of the art of psychotherapy. While both are obviously based upon basic communication skills and one's ability to relate in a meaningful way to others, they are indeed different and require different training formulations and experiences. In fact, some practices of psychotherapy such as paradoxical intention or the infringement upon ego defense mechanisms are clearly contraindicated in crisis intervention.

Salmon (1919) as well as Kardiner and Spiegel (1947) writing about their experiences in world wars regarding emergency psychiatry, note that the emergency provision of care during a crisis is different than traditional clinical applications. From their analyses emerged the three principles of the crisis intervention process:

1) Immediacy - rapid intervention
2) Proximity - close to or within the crisis venue

3) Expectancy - setting appropriate expectations for
   treatment and returning to function.

In a later analysis of crisis intervention within the context of a psychiatric emergency, Slaby and his co-workers (Slaby, Lieb, and Tancredi, 1975) point to the key factors in successful intervention as:

1) Immediacy (i.e., rapid intervention).
2) Innovation (i.e., creative and flexible intervention).
3) Pragmatism (i.e., practical, goal-directed, action oriented intervention. Some might think of this as "common sense.")

In a recent review of psychiatric therapies, Spiegel and Classen (1995) analyzed the processes which undergrid crisis intervention. They are as follows:

1) Immediacy in timing of the intervention,
2) Social support, listening,
3) Ventilation of emotion (catharsis),
4) Commonality of experience as shared by those who participated in the same or similar crisis
5) Cognitive processing of the crisis,
6) Anticipatory guidance (i.e., anticipating for the person in distress),
7) Educating, normalizing, teaching coping responses.

CURATIVE FACTORS IN GROUPS

In the 1960s and 1970s group dynamics and group therapy were popular phenomena of inquiry. One of the most knowledgable of writers and practitioners was Irving Yalom. Yalom (1970) wrote a classic textbook on group therapy. In his text, Yalom reported on a survey that he had conducted where he asked participants in group therapy what the "curative" factors were that facilitated improvement. The factors perceived as most important by Yalom's respondents are as follows, listed in descending order of importance:

1) Interpersonal learning (i.e. learning how to better relate to others and how to integrate information from others)

2) Catharsis (i.e., the ventilation of emotions)

3) Cohesiveness (i.e., relating to and with others in such a manner as to feel an integral part of the group and to identify with the group)

4) Personal insight (i.e., knowledge gained about oneself through introspection and information from others)

5) Interpersonal teaching of others

6) Existential awareness

7) Universality (i.e., destruction of the myth of unique vulnerability or unique weakness)

8) Instillation of hope

All of these factors are potentially active in not just therapy groups, but crisis intervention groups, as well.

FACTORS IN CRISIS INTERVENTION GROUPS

Recognizing the popularity and widespread utilization of crisis intervention groups, Wollman (1993) analyzed the bases for their effectiveness. His findings are as follows:

1) Group cohesion

2) Universality

3) Catharsis

4) Imitative behavior

5) Instillation of hope

6) Imparting of information (teaching)

7) Altruism

8) Timeliness

9) Existential factors

A review of these factors reveals that in Wollman's opinion, crisis intervention groups are effective for many of the same reasons that psychotherapy groups are effective, but with the added advantage of timeliness (i.e., "immediacy" in the language of crisis intervention).

MECHANISMS ACTIVE IN CISD

In an examination of specifically the critical incident stress debriefing (CISD) group crisis intervention technology, Everly (1995a) identified ten putative mechanisms of action (see also Mitchell and Everly, 1995).

1) Early intervention
2) Affective ventilation (catharsis)
3) Opportunity to put the crisis into words on a cognitive level
4) Behavioral structure
5) Psychological structure and progression
6) Yalom's group processes (as noted earlier)
7) Support from one's peers
8) Demonstration of caring
9) Instillation of hope and a sense of control
10) Opportunity for follow-up assessment and treatment, if appropriate.

MECHANISMS ACTIVE IN CISM

It was the famous Johns Hopkins physician, Sir William Osler who said, "To study the phenomenology of medicine without reading . . . is like sailing an unchartered sea."

Having reviewed the specific CISM interventions and the previous literatures, we are in a much better position to speculate upon the mechanisms of action inherent in the CISM approach to crisis response.

As noted earlier behavioral and psychological interventions are not likely to derive their effectiveness from a single monolithic action (referred to as a main effect in analysis of variance parlance). Rather, behavioral and psychological interventions are far more likely to derive their effectiveness from interacting factors, or variables. Thus, they represent interaction effects. As the effects of interacting variables seldom are additive, but are synergistically multiplicative, even rigorous components analyses are seldom capable of ascribing relative weights to interacting variables in a manner that is valid for all individuals. So rather than estimate their relative values, we have simply chosen to offer the following factors as those which we believe are the core process "mechanisms of action" upon which all of CISM, as a crisis response intervention system, rests. They are as follows:

I. Early Intervention

CISM interventions are designed to be implemented during the acute crisis phase, in the form of in-the-field, on-scene support, as well as, as quickly after the acute crisis resolution as possible. There is simply nothing quicker by design. Early, if not immediate, intervention has long been recognized as an important aspect of crisis response.

Salmon (1919) and Kardiner and Spiegel (1947) noted the importance of rapid, emergency-oriented psychiatric intervention in World War I and World War II, respectively.

Lindy's (1985) notion of the trauma membrane argues that after a traumatic event victims begin to "insulate" themselves from the world through the construction of a "trauma membrane," or protective shell. The longer one waits to penetrate the shell, the more difficult it becomes, according to this formulation.

Earlier, Rapoport (1965) argued for the practical importance of early intervention, as did Spiegel and Classen (1995) in their review of emergency psychiatry.

Empirically, Bordow and Porritt (1979) were probably the first to test the importance of early crisis response. Their results support the conclusion that immediate intervention is more effective than delayed intervention.

Soloman and Benbenishty (1986) empirically analyzed the three tenets of crisis response: immediacy, proximity, and expectancy. Each of the three was found to exert a positive effect.

Lastly, Post (1992), in a most provocative paper, argues that early intervention may prevent a genetically-based lowered threshold for neurological excitation from developing in response to trauma. Thus, early intervention may prevent the development of a cellular "memory" of trauma from being transmitted to excitatory neural tissues.

II. The Provision of Psychosocial Support

All human beings require some form of support from others (i.e., psychosocial support). Such support may come in the form of esteem, friendship, respect, trust, aid in problem-solving, or merely listening. Crisis accentuates this need.

American psychologist Carl Rogers wrote cogently in his theory of self psychology that all humans have an innate need for "positive regard" (Rogers, 1951). They possess a need to be valued by others.

Bowlby (1969) argues that there exists a biological drive for the bonding, or attachment, between humans, especially between mother and child.

Similarly, Maslow (1970) has written most coherently that one of the basic human needs is the need for social affiliation with others. According to Maslovian theory, many crises result from a loss of social support / affiliation.

Jerome Frank (1974), in his analysis of psychotherapy, argues that all psychotherapeutic improvement is based on the intervention's ability to reduce demoralization, especially through contradicting the notion of alienation. Individuals in crisis often feel alone, uniquely plagued, and abandoned.

By its very existence, any form of crisis response initiates the process of social support. It contradicts the alienation phenomenon, shows caring, and shows that the person in crisis is valued by others. It also contradicts any sense of abandonment.

The empirical evidence for social support as an effective crisis response tactic is persuasive. Buckley, Blanchard, and Hickling (1996) found an inverse relationship between social support and the prevalence of posttraumatic stress disorder in the wake of motor vehicle accidents. Bunn and Clarke (1979), in an early study of crisis intervention technologies, found that as crisis counseling services were provided, in the form of 20 minutes of supportive counseling, anxiety levels diminished. Dalgleish, and others (1996) also confirmed the assumption that social support is inversely correlated with posttraumatic stress-related symptoms. Finally, Flannery (1990), in a comprehensive review of the role of social support in psychological trauma, found a general trend indicative of the value of social support in reducing the adverse impact of trauma.

III. The Opportunity for Expression

Bruno Bettleheim, an early psychotraumatologist, noted, "What cannot be talked about can also not be put to rest" (Bettleheim, 1984, p. 166). Much earlier, according to van der Hart and his co-workers (van der Hart, Brown, and van der Kolk, 1989) Pierre Janet declared in the late 1800s that successful recovery from trauma required the patient to verbally reconstruct and express the traumatic event.

The notion that recovery from trauma is predicated upon the verbal expression of not only emotions, but also cognitions, is virtually universal throughout crisis response literature. Spiegel and Classen (1995) note the importance of cognitively processing the crisis, in their review of crisis psychiatry.

Pennebaker and his colleagues in an elegant series of empirical investigations demonstrated the true value of expression (Pennebaker, 1985, 1990; Pennebaker and Harber, 1993; Pennebaker and Beall, 1986). His investigations demonstrate the value of expression on, not only psychological outcome measures, but physiological measures and behavioral measures, as well.

IV. Crisis Education: Expectancy and Coping

The fourth and final mechanism of action we find operating in CISM is that of crisis education (i.e., setting appropriate expectations and teaching practical coping techniques).

Persons in crisis commonly experience a sense of being out of control. Recovery (i.e., the restoration of psychological homeostasis) is often dependent upon reestablishing a sense of control. The perception of control is enhanced through setting appropriate expectations and teaching effective instrumental coping behaviors (Everly, 1989; Bandura, 1997).

Investigations and formulations by Taylor (1983) and Bandura (1997) argue convincingly for the power of perceived control as a mitigator of crisis stress, and psychological discord. In his review of control and stress, Everly (1989) concludes that understanding, as induced by information / education is a powerful stress reduction strategy. Further, Spiegel and Classen (1995) point out that cognitive processing of the crisis is also an important step toward resolution. Thus, the operational corollaries of these formulations would be educational interventions so as to:

1) warn people in high risk environments as to the nature of their risk exposure and how to cope with crisis situations if they do occur (Hytten and Hasle, 1989; Weisaeth, 1989; Jonsson, 1995) as is done in pre-crisis preparation protocols (Backman, et al., 1997; Mitchell and Everly, 1996); and

2) teach crisis coping techniques during the crisis as a means of mitigating the crisis response, facilitating reestablishment of homeostasis, and increasing the sense of self-efficacy (Bandura, 1997; Everly, 1989).

SUMMARY

In this chapter, we have reviewed the concepts and mechanisms that are thought to serve as a foundation for CISM as a crisis response system. In the final analysis we have concluded that four fundamental elements, or processes, are present:

1) Early intervention

2) The provision of psychosocial support

3) The opportunity for expression

4) Crisis education:

    a) Cognitive processing

    b) Behavioral coping responses

Recalling to mind the reviews of Salmon (1919) Kardiner and Spiegel (1947), Spiegel and Classen (1995), Frank (1974), Slaby, Lieb, and Tancredi (1975), and even Yalom (1970) we find that the CISM formulation has incorporated the most fundamental of all these therapeutic process analyses. Indeed, the search for mechanisms of action in psychological interventions is not an easy one. That which is most florid, is not always that which is most salient. Often times the most potent mechanisms are latent, or obscured. In our opinion the most potent and fundamental factors in crisis response are the elements of:

1) Early intervention,

2) Psychosocial support,

3) The opportunity for expression, and

4) Education (i.e., cognitive processing, setting appropriate expectations and teaching adaptive behavioral coping).

Thus these four factors are, we believe, the four cornerstones of CISM.

CHAPTER SEVEN

CISM: A Review of Effectiveness

In previous chapters, we have described the comprehensive CISM approach to crisis response and the mechanisms inherent in CISM that are most likely accountable for its effectiveness. But what of an assessment of the overall effectiveness of CISM? Indeed, what do we know about the ability of the CISM approach to achieve positive outcome? In this chapter, we shall address the effectiveness of CISM as a crisis response technology.

DEFINING EFFECTIVENESS

CISM is a variant of what has been known historically as crisis intervention (Greenstone, 1993). Elementary and monolithic crisis intervention programs have been in existence since the 1950s and they persist today. The proponents of crisis intervention theory and application base their support largely upon anecdotal empiricism and case studies. Investigators who support the application of crisis intervention technologies most typically point to acute effectiveness as the index of success or failure. Indeed, any intervention approach within the crisis response genre should first and foremost provide some mitigation of acute psychological distress. By way of analogy, as physical first aid is to surgery, crisis response (including CISM) is to psychotherapy. Thus, crisis response has been referred to as "emotional first aid" and therefore should be evaluated, not as a psychotherapy capable of cure, but rather primarily as an emotional first-aid technique capable of mitigation and secondary prevention.

DEFINING CISM

The essence of the CISM approach to crisis response is the utilization of an integrated multifactorial multicomponent program which spans the crisis / trauma spectrum from pre-crisis preparation through post-crisis intervention and follow-up. Therefore, our review of CISM effectiveness:

1) will review *only* those programs which are consistent with the "Mitchell model" formulations of CISD and CISM (Mitchell and Everly, 1996), as prescribed in this volume. To review other crisis response formulations would inappropriately dilute the review with ambiguous heterogeneity (i.e., "mix apples and oranges,") serving to further add to the confusion which already characterizes this field. One would certainly not review all styles of psychotherapy if interested in only one particular psychotherapeutic school, or formulation, and

2) must focus primarily upon those programs which utilize the integrated multifactorial and / or multicomponent nature of CISM, as prescribed in this volume and elsewhere (Mitchell and Everly, 1996).

The Essence of CISM - The utilization of an integrated comprehensive mulitfactorial, multicomponent program for crisis response which spans the crisis spectrum, from pre-crisis preparation through post-crisis intervention, and follow-up.

So, as we address the question of CISM effectiveness, we must review investigations which serve to answer the question at hand, which includes:

1) research which focuses upon the effectiveness of the "Mitchell model" CISD intervention as a commonly utilized historical foundation of the more comprehensive CISM approach;

2) research which examines the effectiveness of multifactorial CISM-like interventions programs which closely approximate the comprehensive CISM approach, as prescribed herein; and

3) research which examines the effectiveness of the more comprehensive, multicomponent CISM approach to crisis response, as prescribed in this volume and elsewhere (Mitchell and Everly, 1996).

VALIDITY OF DESIGN

Historically, behavioral science knowledge was based upon data generated from well-controlled efficacy research. Efficacy research typically used randomized experimental designs with one or more control groups contrasted against an experimental group. Research designs which used nonrandomized assignment to experimental and control groups, as well as survey research was viewed as being of minimal value to the conduct of inquiry. These issues have traditionally plagued the field psychotherapy research, and, of course, the field of crisis response.

Recently, noted psychologist and president of the American Psychological Association Dr. Martin Seligman (Seligman, 1995) has argued cogently for the power of nonrandomized experimental and even survey research designs. He notes,

> "I no longer believe that efficacy studies are the only, or even the best, way of finding out what treatments actually work in the field. I have come

to believe that the 'effectiveness' study of how patients fare under the actual conditions . . . in the field, can yield . . . 'empirical validation' (Seligman, 1995, p. 966).

Seligman (1995) goes on to conclude, "Random assignment . . . may turn out to be worse than useless for the investigation of the actual treatment of mental illness in the field" (p. 974). He reaches this conclusion based upon the belief that efficacy studies are simply the wrong method for such research because they omit too many of the crucial elements that characterize what is actually done in the field; for example, the level of competence of the interventionist, the real-time self-correcting nature of the intervention, the complex and nature of precipitating stressors.

Similarly, it is important to keep in mind that randomized designs do not eliminate selection or assignment error, they simply serve to diminish the likelihood of systematic error. The effects of randomization may be approximated through the measurement of potential sources of systematic error, the use of large sample sizes drawn from diverse constituencies, and even meta-analytic approaches.

As we review research on CISD/CISM, the reader will see a wide variety of designs ranging from survey research and quasi-experimental, to forms of randomized assignment research.

RESEARCH ON CISD ONLY

In this section, we shall examine research investigations on the singular application of the "Mitchell model" CISD intervention as it serves as a frame of reference for the historical development of CISM.

Historically, survey research has been dismissed as being of little value in the conduct of inquiry due to its lack of standardized controls. Seligman (1995), on the other hand, has argued that large scale, self-report survey research has a low likelihood of possessing systematic error. Thus, self-report survey data may contribute in a meaningful manner to the issue of effectiveness.

The first three studies in this section employ survey designs.

Robyn Robinson and Jeffrey Mitchell (1993) used a survey designed to assess the effectiveness of one the CISM interventions, CISD. Participants in the study consisted of 288 Australian emergency services, welfare and hospital personnel who had taken part in 31 CISDs from December 1987 through August 1989. Responses were received from 172 (60%) of the surveyed group. Ninety six percent of the emergency services personnel and 77% of the welfare and hospital personnel reported a reduction in crisis-related symptoms due, in part, to CISD.

In a study of 219 nurses, 193 reported that the CISD process had been personally helpful to them (Burns and Harm, 1993).

The Association of Orthopaedic Surgeons conducted a survey of 436 emergency medical responders to assess their personal experience with CISD. Of the 350 who participated in a CISD, 314 (90.8%) responded that the CISD was "beneficial" (AAOS, 1996).

Not all CISD research employs survey designs. Several studies have investigated the effectiveness of the CISD intervention using various control group designs.

In an investigation of the CISD intervention, Bohl (1991) assessed the mandatory CISD upon law enforcement officers who had experienced a critical incident. The effectiveness of the CISD was assessed three months post-incident utilizing standardized written psychometrics. Officers who had received the CISD within 24 hours of the incident (n = 40) were compared to officers who received no CISD (n = 31). Those who received the CISD were found to be less depressed, less angry, and to possess fewer stress-related symptoms. Bohl's description of the control and experimental groups argues against evidence of systematic error in subject assignment and for a naturalistic randomization process.

On October 16, 1991 a mass shooting in a crowded cafeteria in Killeen, Texas left 55 people wounded; 23 people would die of their wounds. Emergency medical personnel from two local fire / rescue departments responded to this mass fatality incident. The state of Texas provided voluntary CISDs for the rescue personnel within 24 hours after the shooting. A total of 36 respondents participated in this longitudinal assessment of the effectiveness of the CISD interventions (Jenkins, 1996). Recovery from the trauma appeared to be most strongly associated with participation in the CISD process. CISD was useful in reducing symptoms of depression and anxiety for those who participated in the CISD compared to those who did not. The authors make a special point in indicating that this study addresses many of the common methodological problems existing in the debriefing literature, as described by Bisson and Deahl (1994).

Ogden Rogers authored a doctoral dissertation entitled *An Examination of Critical Incident Stress Debriefing for Emergency Services Providers: A Quasi-Experimental Field Study*. He also evaluated the "Mitchell model" debriefing and states in his research summary that data were analyzed using qualitative and multiple regression techniques. The analysis suggests that the CISD process was helpful in reducing psychosocial stress by generating a moderate increase in a feeling of being in control of one's reactions to the critical incident. In this dissertation, 72% of the emergency personnel who received debriefings reported lowered symptoms after the debriefing. Dr. Rogers reports that there are small " . . . significant increases in resolution in persons who participated in the debriefing process, when controlling for other presumed influencing variables" and that on " . . . the resolution of stress as measured by the Critical Incident Resolution Scale . . . Mean scores for the participant sample are 1.06 times greater than the nonparticipant sample" (Rogers, 1993, p. 71; 77).

The CISD intervention has found application not only in well circumscribed critical incidents, but mass disasters, as well. The CISD protocol was used subsequent to Hurricane Iniki for 41 crisis response personnel on the island of Kauai. The research cohort was divided into two groups for pre-test and post-test comparisons (Chemtob, et al., 1996). To provide a control group paradigm, a time-lagged design was employed wherein the pre-treatment assessment of the second group was concurrent with the post-treatment assessment of the first group. Repeated ANOVA indicated that psychometrically assessed posttraumatic stress (Impact of Events Scale) was reduced in both groups as a result of the CISD intervention.

After the Los Angeles riots in 1992 researchers studied the impact of stress reactions on emergency medical services personnel and the effectiveness of CISD. Using the Frederick Reaction Index the researchers compared groups of emergency medical services personnel who had received debriefings with those who had not received the service after the same or very similar experiences in the riots. Those workers who were given an opportunity to participate in a critical incident stress debriefing session scored significantly lower on the Frederick Reaction Index compared to those not offered this service (Wee, Mills and Koehler, 1993; Wee, 1996).

Wee's data argues for the absence of systematic assignment error, thus supporting the notion of naturalistic randomization in assignment for those who utilized the CISD compared to those who did not.

Lastly, in 1994, Scandinavia suffered its worst peacetime sea disaster in history with the sinking of the Estonia. Over 900 people perished. Nurmi (1997) contrasted three groups of emergency response personnel who received the CISD intervention with a group of emergency nurses who received support from their supervisors, but no CISD. Nurmi contrasted 38 frontier guards, 30 firefighters, and 26 disaster victim identification team members to 28 emergency room nurses. Data indicated that psychometrically assessed (Impact of Events Scale) symptoms of posttraumatic stress disorder several days post incident were lower in each of the three groups that received the CISD. Nurmi notes that this was the largest application of "Mitchell model" in Finnish history.

MULTIFACTORIAL CISM-LIKE PROGRAMS

Multifactorial CISM-like crisis response programs contain most, or all, of the CISM intervention concepts, but may not be thought of as CISM or referred to as CISM.

Somewhat prior to the current authors' formulations of CISM, the notion of an integrated multifactorial crisis intervention program was assessed in Australia. Bordow and Porritt (1979) employed a 3-group design contrasting 1) no intervention to 2) a one session "review" of facts and emotions, to 3) a multifactorial CISM-like intervention for victims of traffic traumas. The results of this random assignment investigation indicated that a one session crisis intervention was effective in the reduction of adverse effects of trauma, but further analysis revealed that the integrated multifactorial intervention was even more effective.

In a 1982 study of Israeli soldiers Solomon and Benbenishty (1986) investigated the core crisis intervention principles of proximity, immediacy, and expectancy. Their investigation revealed that all three were positively correlated with returning to the fighting unit. Further analyses revealed that immediacy and expectancy were correlated inversely with the development of posttraumatic stress disorder.

In support of the multifactorial integrated CISM-like approach to crisis response, the authors conclude, "The effects of proximity, immediacy, and expectancy seem to be interrelated . . . the findings of this study clearly demonstrate the cumulative effect of implementing all three treatment principles" (Solomon and Benbenishty, 1986, p. 616).

Brom, Kleber, and Hofman (1993) conducted an investigation of the primary victims of traffic trauma. A group of 83 subjects were randomly assigned to the intervention group. The intervention itself consisted of a CISM-like three program which combined "practical help," "information," "support," "reality testing," "confrontation with the experience," and "referral to psychotherapeutic treatment." While scores on the Impact of Events Scale failed to demonstrate differences between the monitoring control group and the experimental group, scores on the checklist of trauma symptoms did, indeed, show the effectiveness of the multifactorial CISM-like intervention.

COMPREHENSIVE CISM PROGRAMS

The following studies have investigated CISM programs as prescribed in the volume.

In an early CISM investigation, Marsha Leeman-Conley (1990) assessed the CISM approach to crisis as it was applied to the Commonwealth Banking Corporation in Australia in response to the trauma of hold-ups. Leeman-Conley used the bank as its own control comparing outcome data before and after a CISM program, as prescribed in this volume, was instituted. Her data are striking. While the number of hold-ups actually increased from 30 to 38, comparing the control interval to the experimental interval, the number of bank staff sick days directly attributed to the hold-ups were seen to decline by 60%. Similarly, other sick days were seen to decline by 60% within six months of the hold-ups when the CISM program was in place. Finally, workers' compensation payment were seen to decline by 68% after the CISM program was initiated.

The On Site Academy in Gardner, Massachusetts is a residential rehabilitation program for individuals who have experienced psychologically disabling symptoms from some form of traumatic experience. The On Site Academy's constituency is the emergency services personnel of North America. The Academy employs a short-term residential variation of the CISM program. A rationale for such utilization is that for these individuals, so adversely affected by trauma, they still find themselves in the midst of a psychological crisis, regardless of how much time has actually passed since the actual traumatization. The core components of the Academy's CISM program are:

- Training / education into the nature of stress, trauma and crisis coping techniques
- CISD
- Paraprofessional peer support
- Individual counseling (at least 3 sessions)
- Eye Movement Desensitization and Reprocessing (EMDR)

In an evaluation of the On Site Academy's program, Manzi (1995) surveyed 108 participants and gained a response of 45 returned surveys (41.7%). The average amount of time respondents had been out of the program was ten months.

Program participants were surveyed to inquire if the Academy's CISM program had met their expectations and goals;

100% indicated that it had. Further, 100% of the surveyed participants indicated they would recommend the Academy.

Further survey inquiry was made to assess the effectiveness of the Academy's CISM program in reducing trauma related symptoms. Participants were asked to indicate, using symptom checklists, their symptomatic response to a traumatic event prior to entering the Academy's program. They were then asked to indicate their current symptom response after completing the Academy's program. Symptoms were assessed, using this retrospective pretest posttest design, in four domains: cognitive, emotional, behavioral, and physiologic. The investigation by Manzi (1995) revealed significant decreases in all four symptom domains from pre-CISM to post-CISM.

Following a successful pilot project on nursing stress (Kirwin, 1994) in the Manitoba region of Canada, the Medical Services Branch authorized the implementation of a national CISM program for the Indian and Northern Health Services nurses. A full CISM program was implemented. Subsequently these nurses were sampled to assess both the need and the effectiveness of the CISM program.

Survey and interview data were collected, analyzed, and reviewed by an independent evaluation organization (Westen Management Consultants, 1996). Data were collected from nurses working in Pacific / British Columbia, Alberta, Manitoba, and Ontario. Of 582 nurses, 236 responded (41%).

As for need, the study revealed that 65% of the nurses experience at least one critical incident per year in the workplace. These critical incidents included, but were not limited to:

- Death of a child - 37% of nurses
- Attempted or actual physical assault - 28%
- Break-ins at nursing facilities - 25%

- Verbal threats / assaults - 52%
- Suicide or attempted suicide of a patient - 44%

The CISM concept was operationalized and instituted as a means of reducing critical incident - related stress and discord. Some the results are summarized below:

- 82% of field nurses who had used CISM services reported that the services met or exceeded their expectations
- 89% of field nurses indicated they were satisfied with the CISM services
- 99% of the field nurses indicated that the CISM program reduced the number of days they were absent from work

The evaluation report (Western Management Consultants, 1996) concluded, "Survey data suggest MSB CISM significantly reduced turnover among field nurses" (p. 53). As many as 24% of the nurses who experienced a critical incident contemplated leaving their jobs, but did not after a CISM intervention. It was estimated that it would cost CN $38,000 to replace a single nurse.

Further financial evaluations revealed a 7.09 financial benefit-to-cost ratio which may be seen as over 700% return on investment. The authors of the evaluation report concluded, "It is evident that the quality of the existing program is exceptional. The MSB program is a state-of-the-art program that should be emulated by other employers, and sets a standard by which alternatives should be judged" (Western Management Consultants, 1996, p. iv).

The MSB CISM program is virtually a prototypic CISM program as prescribed by this volume.

The Los Angeles County Fire Department (LACoFD) has one of the oldest emergency services CISM programs in existence, having been initiated in 1986 in the wake of the Cerritos air disaster. Since that time over 500 CISDs have been implemented and a full CISM program ultimately established.

The LACoFD's CISM program was evaluated through the dissemination of 3000 research surveys (Hokanson, 1997). Of the 3000 disseminated, 2124 were completed for a 70.8% return rate. Of the 2124 respondents, over 600 indicated that they had participated in a Critical Incident Stress Debriefing (CISD).

As noted by Hokanson (1997), two of explicitly stated goals of the CISM program are:

1) to accelerate the recovery process after a traumatic event and

2) to reduce the adverse impact of a traumatic event.

The LACoFD data strongly support the effectiveness of the CISM program in achieving both of these goals (Hokanson, 1997). More specifically:

1) The CISD process was shown to be effective in accelerating the recovery process in response to traumatic events:

a) 56.3% of respondents experienced a significant reduction of trauma-related symptoms within 72 hours after the CISD, compared to 45.5% indicating reduction of symptoms without the CISD in response to a comparable traumatic event. Thus the 72 hour incremental recovery utility for CISD was 10.8% beyond the natural recovery process.

b) 74.1% of respondents experienced a significant reduction of trauma-related symptoms within one week after the CISD, compared to 65.5% indicating reduction of symptoms without the CISD in response to a comparable traumatic event. Thus, the one-week incremental recovery utility for CISD was 8.6%.

Such findings have implications for medical utilization, sick leave, and workers compensation claims.

2) The CISD process was shown to be effective in facilitating the amelioration of trauma-related symptoms. Of the respondents, only 13.9% indicated they had persistent trauma-related symptoms more than 6 months post-trauma and post-CISD, compared to 16.5% indicating persistent symptoms in response to a comparable trauma wherein no CISD was affected. Thus, the incremental recovery utility was 2.6% for the CISD in this analysis.

Such findings have implications for workers' compensation disability claims and the incidence of early retirement and general turnover.

Finally, Flannery and his coworkers (Flannery, et al., 1991, 1995; Flannery and Penk, 1996) conducted a series of elegant studies testing the concept of multidimensional critical incident stress management as applied to workplace violence in three state mental hospitals. Each hospital created a critical incident response team using solid CISM principles, including CISD. The cumulative results of this well controlled multi-site study yielded strong evidence for the ability of CISM to reduce the harmful effects of workplace violence. Reduced sick leave, accident claims and staff turnover were reported as a result of CISM program.

SUMMARY

In this chapter, we have reviewed a wide array of studies which assess the effectiveness of CISM as we have developed and described this approach to crisis response.

We have divided the studies into three groups: 1) CISD, 2) CISM-like multifactorial interventions, and 3) comprehensive CISM. Table 7.1 summarizes our review.

Table 7.1		
Research on CISD / CISM Effectiveness		
CISD	**MULTIFACTORIAL CISM-LIKE**	**COMPREHENSIV CISM**
Robinson & Mitchell (1993)	Bordow & Porritt (1979)	Leeman-Conley (199
Burns & Harm (1993)	Solomon & Benbenishty (1986)	Manzi (1995)
AAOS (1996)	Brom, Kleber, & Hofman (1993)	WMC (1996)
Bohl (1991)		Hokanson (1997)
Jenkins (1996)		Flannery, et al. (199
Rogers (1993)		1995, 199(
Chemtob, et al., (1996)		
Wee, et al., (1996)		
Nurmi, (1997)		

In addition, Mitchell and Everly (1997) have taken broader approach to the review of CISM effectiveness exam both the theoretical and empirical foundations for the (approach to crisis response.

While the studies reviewed in this chapter provide v degrees of support for the CISM approach, a study by Hytt Hasle (1989) found no significant effect for debriefing in a s 58 nonprofessional firefighters in Norway subsequent to a major hotel fire. Similarly, Deahl, et al., (1994) found no difference in British soldiers who were debriefed contrasted to those who were not debriefed subsequent to the Gulf War. Kenardy et al (1996) compared 62 rescue workers who were debriefed in response to symptoms was observed between the two groups. Finally, while

Erratum - p. 87 (bottom of page)

Kenardy, et al. (1996) compared 62 rescue workers who were debriefed in response to the Newcastle, Australia earthquake, to 133 rescue workers who were not debriefed. No difference in symptoms was observed between the two groups.

McFarlane found short-term effectiveness for debriefings in 469 firefighters in Australia, long-term effectiveness was called into question as neuroticism interacted with debriefing attendance to predict subsequent psychiatric symptoms.

These studies were not a part of our primary review due to the fact these studies failed to utilize "Mitchell model" CISD/CISM formulations and therefore were inappropriate for inclusion, as was a study by Bunn and Clarke (1979) which found a more positive effect for crisis intervention technologies. Thus, in order to answer the question of CISM effectiveness we must assess only those studies which do indeed utilize CISM technologies as described herein.

Both Bisson and Deahl (1994) and Robinson and Mitchell (1995) provide useful reviews of the methodological problems in crisis intervention, debriefing, and CISM research.

CHAPTER EIGHT

CISM and Issues of Standards of Care

Early in this volume, we raised the issue of standards of care. To reiterate, a standard of care refers to a generally recognized and accepted procedure, intervention, or pattern of practice. It serves to set the minimal expectations for service provision. As such, it has implications for forensic settings in that issues of negligence, denial of reasonable and expected care, and clinical malpractice are typically defined according to the barometer of standards of care.

Seldom are standards of care instantly acknowledged or "anointed," rather standards of care often evolve from the contexts of industry practices and / or community practices.

In this chapter, we shall examine CISM as standard of care in crisis intervention and emergency mental health services.

GOVERNMENTAL GUIDELINES

Both state and federal governmental agencies have recognized the importance of providing psychological support subsequent to crises and traumatic stressors at the workplace. Let us take a closer look at their responses to these hazards.

The state of California has taken the lead in mandating psychological support subsequent to crisis events.

The California Occupational Safety and Health Administration has mandated guidelines for workplace security. It notes, "Effective security management to prevent all three types of workplace violence events . . . includes post-event measures such as emergency medical care and debriefing employees about the incident" (Cal-OSHA, 1994, p. 13).

Similarly, the state of California has mandated that CISM-like services be provided for health care and community service workers. Their safety guidelines state: "A trauma-crisis counseling or critical incident debriefing program must be established and provided on an on-going basis . . . In addition, peer counseling or support programs may be provided" (Dept. Industrial Relations, 1993, p. 24).

As described above, we see that the state of California has mandated CISM-like programs to protect the health and welfare of its citizens in the wake of workplace violence. While the federal government has not mandated such programs, it has recommended CISM-like programs while making compliance voluntary at this point.

In *Guidelines for Preventing Workplace Violence for Health Care and Social Service Workers* - OSHA 3148-1996, the Occupational Safety and Health Administration indicates:

> "Management commitment, including endorsement and visible involvement of top management, provides the motivations and resources to deal effectively with workplace violence, should include the following:
> . . . A comprehensive program of medical and psychological counseling and debriefing for employees experiencing or witnessing assaults and other violent incidents" (OSHA, 1996, p. 4).

As workplace violence escalates to epidemic proportions, the National Institute of Occupational Safety and Health (NIOSH) has also initiated recommended guidelines for the safety of the workforce.

According to NIOSH Bulletin 57 (NIOSH, 1996), it is recommended that workplace violence policies and prevention programs be initiated. According to NIOSH,

> " A comprehensive workplace violence prevention policy and program should . . . include procedures and responsibilities to be taken in the event of a violent incident in the workplace. This policy should explicitly state how the response team is to be assembled and who is responsible for immediate care of the victim(s), reestablishing work areas and processes, and organizing and carrying out stress debriefing sessions with victims, their coworkers, and perhaps the families of victims and coworkers" (NIOSH, 1996, p. 16).

Thus, we see that the state government of California, as well as the Federal Government, urge employers to establish "comprehensive" psychological support programs, including debriefings, for employees who experience traumas at the workplace. The CISM program as described in this volume not only represents such a comprehensive, integrated program as is recommended by these governmental agencies, but its existence has undeniably done much to foster these recommendations.

AMERICAN RED CROSS

In 1991, the American Red Cross created a bold initiative to provide mental health services in response to disasters (ARC, 1991). Their programs are designed to serve both primary victims as well as Red Cross workers themselves. Drawing partially upon the work of Jeffrey T. Mitchell, they formulated a mental health intervention program consistent with the guidelines of a CISM program as noted in this volume.

The Red Cross recognizes four mental health interventions:
1. Defusings
2. Debriefings
3. Crisis counseling
4. Crisis intervention

CISM AS A STANDARD OF CARE

As noted earlier in this volume, we present the core concepts of CISM for consideration as a standard of care within the context of emergency mental health and crisis intervention services. Very simply, we believe that crisis intervention and related services, in the workplace and elsewhere, should be conceived of as, and implemented within, a comprehensive multicomponent, integrated program of services. Our term for this is Critical Incident Stress Management (CISM). Such a program should span the full crisis spectrum from the pre-crisis preparation and training phase, acute crisis on-scene support, through post-crisis intervention and referral for formal mental health assessment and treatment, if appropriate. The CISM program is operationally described by Mitchell and Everly, (1996).

The CISM concept has already been implicitly and / or explicitly embraced, as well as widely implemented, as noted by the plethora of recommendations, mandatory guidelines, and actual CISM and CISM-like programs detailed in this volume. There currently exists a network of over 300 CISM crisis response teams in North America associated with International Critical Incident Stress Foundation, Inc. In point of fact numerous state governments have already established divisions of CISM. As described earlier, a standard of care need not necessarily be officially and universally declared, it can simply evolve from a community and / or industry pattern of practice. Clearly, it may be argued that CISM has evolved into a standard of care based upon its recognition and utilization across numerous and diverse venues within the context of emergency mental health and crisis response services. Such recognition and utilization arguably makes it the most widely used formal crisis response system in the world.

CONCLUSION

According to OSHA General Duty Clause 29 USC 1900 5 (a) (1), employers are **required** to provide a safe and healthful working environment for all workers covered by the OSHA Act of 1970. The CISM program represents one approach to achieving that goal by acknowledging and responding to the psychological risks and hazards of the workplace. Not only do CISM services make sense from a humanitarian perspective, they make sense from a business perspective, as well. CISM programs may serve to reduce the adversarial environment that sometimes surrounds crisis oriented occupations. For example, a deputy sheriff in Montana suffered a psychological disability as a result of his work. The perceived lack of an adequate crisis response program caused him to sue his employer for not providing adequate psychological support in response to his work-related trauma. The lawsuit was settled after six years. The settlement was in excess of $200,000. While we have no "hard" data on the number of lawsuits avoided by CISM programs, we have heard time after time anecdotally, about the spirit of cooperation, the respect and the concern for people that is communicated by the mere existence of CISM-like programs, either at the workplace or in the community.

In the final analysis, its people are this country's most valuable resource. CISM programs are designed to protect and enhance that resource and in doing so may emerge as the minimally acceptable response to crisis and trauma, that is, a "standard of care."

Special Considerations in Critical Incident Stress Management

APPENDIX A:

The Crisis Response Team: Guidelines for Team Development

APPENDIX A:

The Crisis Response (CISM) Team:
General Guidelines for Team Development

STEP 1:   Identify the need for the crisis response (CISM) team. Based upon identified needs, a rationale for the team's existence should both pragmatically and rhetorically emerge.

STEP 2:   Clearly state the goals of the crisis response team. Clearly state the constituency to be served by the team.

STEP 3:   Delineate guidelines for team membership and the specific roles to be performed.
- Administrative structure
- Dispatching functions
- Response functions, listing mental health providers' roles vis-a-vis the use of paraprofessionals (if applicable)
- Clinical mental health oversight / supervision
- Team member selection criteria

STEP 4:   Determine how the team will be legally constituted.

STEP 5:   Determine how the team will be funded.

STEP 6: Obtain legal counsel to operationally define issues such as malpractice, standards of care, confidentiality, "good samaritan" practices, necessary liability insurance coverages, etcetera.

STEP 7: Determine what criteria and mechanisms will be used to activate the team. Determine what backup systems will be used in the case of a mass disaster or widespread communication failure.

STEP 8: Determine what specific crisis intervention techniques will be used by the team (For example: defusing, CISD, individual crisis counseling, etc.)

STEP 9: Determine what criteria and mechanisms will be used to deactivate the team.

STEP 10: Stipulate guidelines and procedures for follow-up for team members after a crisis response.

STEP 11: Make arrangements for ongoing "inservice" training.

STEP 12: Create a clear, practical operating manual which contains policies and procedures and which addresses all of the aforementioned issues.

APPENDIX B:

Common Events That May Trigger Activation of a CISM Team and Possible Response Guidelines

APPENDIX B:

Common Events That May Trigger Activation of a CISM Team and Possible Response Guidelines

There are innumerable critical incidents which could trigger a Critical Incident Stress Management response. They may vary somewhat from organization to organization and from community to community. No list could ever encompass all of the distressing crisis events which could happen in the workplace or in a community. There are, however, some common elements about the events and about the people who experience them which might be of assistance in planning the appropriate response to a traumatic event.

1. The events are usually sudden in onset and relatively short in duration. They generally contain an element of surprise or shock. People are frequently unprepared for the crisis, and, even when they are prepared, they are overcome by the intensity of the incident.

2. Traumatic events typically cause significant emotional reactions in those who experience or witness them (APA, 1980). Much of the reaction to a traumatic event depends on the personal view of the situation which is taken by those involved (Everly, 1993).

3. The longer the exposure to the event the more potential there is that harm can be done to those involved.

4. The greater the level of involvement in a traumatic event the greater the potential for harm in those involved or witnessing the event.

5. People who are untrained and ill prepared for a traumatic event tend to have a more serious impact from the experience.

6. Young children and the elderly seem to be more vulnerable to traumatic incidents than do people in other age brackets.

7. The same traumatic event can produce very different reactions in those involved. Some may be unaffected. Others will be overcome with distress. Some may delay their reactions until things calm down around them. The focus of attention should be on those who are showing signals that they are most distressed.

8. No one type of support can be appropriate for all people under all circumstances. A systematic, comprehensive, and multicomponent approach to Critical Incident Stress Management is required to assure maximal recovery of distressed people.

9. One of the most important factors in the recovery of traumatized people, and is a hallmark of the CISM approach to crisis response, is choosing the best type of intervention, at the best time, for the the specific target population requiring crisis response.

Before anything is done with individuals or groups which might be traumatized, three important assessment questions should be answered. These questions are all interrelated and should be considered together as decisions are being made to intervene in a crisis. They are:

Target? Who needs assistance? Involvement in a crisis situation does not necessarily mean that everyone is affected by it. Some may be just fine without intervention. Others may need a minor level of intervention. Others need much more. People trained in the emergency services often need less support than those who are not involved in the emergency services.

It is important to determine if the majority of the group is affected or if only one or two individuals are impacted. It is also important to determine who among those involved is displaying the most serious signs of distress. They should become primary targets of intervention.

On occasion, decisions may be made to include everyone in an intervention even though some may not be seriously affected by the crisis situation.

Timing? When does a CISM team go to work? If the timing of the intervention is off, the intervention will likely fail or be considerably less effective even if people need the support and if the support team picks the proper intervention.

Too much help too early disrupts people's thinking and dampens their effective personal management of the situation. It also produces anger toward the intervention team. If a CISM team is rejected because of an over enthusiastic response to those involved in a crisis, it becomes difficult to convince those involved that later additional support is beneficial.

A delayed response to people in crisis produces an atmosphere of mistrust and discouragement. They may also reject assistance as too little, too late. Proper training and supervised experience helps CISM team members to develop the proper sense of timing for the various interventions.

Type? The right kind of intervention is as important as the proper timing and choosing the people who need assistance. CISM is not made up of only one intervention such as the Critical Incident Stress Debriefing (CISD). Very different interventions exist to fit the circumstances of the crisis event. At times individual support is going to be the best and at other times group work will be indicated. Sometimes the family members of those involved in a crisis will need more assistance than those actually involved. Adaptation and accommodation of specific interventions to fit the circumstances is essential to deliver the best help to those who need it.

Training and experience, as pointed out above, are crucial elements in developing a crisis response team which can appropriately respond to people needs in a timely manner.

Table B.1 reviews common trigger events and possible response options.

Event	Target	Timing	Type *

| *level 1* - events which affect community members but not emergency personnel. |

EXAMPLES:

Event	Target	Timing	Type *
small plane crash in neighborhood one death, no injuries, minor damage	• witnesses • community	• immediate	• individual one-on-one support • community meeting
robbery with no violence	• witnesses	• immediate	• individual one-on-one support • referrals if necessary
	• employees	• immediate	• individual one-on-one support
		• 1-12 hrs.	• defusing • referrals if necessary
		• days later	• CISD • referral

| *level 2* - events which affect community members and a few emergency personnel. |

EXAMPLES:

Event	Target	Timing	Type *
baby death (SIDS)	• family	• immediate	• family crisis support
		• days-weeks later	• referral
	• EMS or police	• immediate	• individual one-on-one support or one helper to a small group

* Note: Individual one-on-one crisis support can be appropriate at any time after a traumatic event, from moments to years post-trauma, whenever recollections of the event or its symptoms overwhelm the individual.

Event	Target	Timing	Type *
	• EMS or police	• 1-12 hrs.	• defusing if not improved by one-on-one support
		• days later	• CISD • referral
	• community	• immediate	• individual one-on-one support
		• few days	• community meeting • referrals if necessary
	• police officer	• immediate	• individual one-on-one support
		• immediate	• medical evaluation if required
		• 1-12 hrs	• individual one-on-one support • referral, if necessary
		• few days	• individual one-on-one support • referral, if necessary
	• other officers	• 1-12 hrs	• defusing
	• all involved police	• few days	• CISD if still necessary after defusing • follow up as necessary

level 3 - significant events with serious affects for victims, community and emergency workers.

EXAMPLES:

fatal auto accident with children involved	• bystanders	• immediate	• individual one-on-one support • referrals, if necessary
		• days later	• referral

Event	Target	Timing	Type *
	• victims	• immediate	• individual one-on-one support • social service support • referral
		• weeks later	• referral
	• fire, rescue, EMS, police, communications officers	• immediate • immediate	• on-scene • various on-scene support services
		• 1-12 hrs. • few days	• defusing • CISD
			• follow up services as necessary
line of duty injury in worksite	• witnesses	• immediate	• individual one-on-one support • referrals, as required
		• 1-12 hrs.	• defusing
		• few days	• CISD
		• next few days	• follow up referrals if required
		• weeks	• referral
	remainder of organization	• 1-12 hrs	• defusing • referrals as required
	if emergency personnel injured	• immediate	• various on scene support services
		• 1-8 hrs • few days	• defusing • CISD • significant other support
		• next few days	• follow up services
			• referrals if necessary
		• weeks	• referral

Event	Target	Timing	Type *

level 4 - a major event with severe impact on victims, community and emergency personnel.			

EXAMPLES:

Event	Target	Timing	Type *
disaster	• primary victims	• immediate	• individual one-on-one support
		• few days - few weeks	• social support services
		• weeks-months	• referral
	• secondary victims and community groups	• within 24 hrs	• community education meeting
		• days -weeks	• identify those needing additional support
		• weeks-months	• referral
	• emergency personnel	• immediate	• various on-scene support interventions
			• demobilization • individual one-on-one support
		• few days	• individual one-on-one support • significant other support services
		• few days to few weeks	• CISD • referrals as required • follow up support services
		• few weeks or more	• referral
line of duty deaths	• witnesses	• immediate	• individual one-on-one support
		• 1-8 hrs	• defusing

Event	Target	Timing	Type *
		• few days	• CISD
		• next few days	• follow up referrals as required
		• weeks	• follow up referrals as required
	• remainder of organization	• within 24 hrs	• information meeting identify those needing support
			• individual one-on-one support
			• referrals as required
	• if emergency personnel involved	• immediate	• various on scene support services
			• individual one-on-one support
		• 1-8 hrs	• day one line of duty death CISD (shortened 5 phase version)
			• individual one-on-one support
		• few days	• individual one-on-one support
			• significant other support
			• CISD for significant others
		• 3-7 days post funeral	• CISD (7 phases)
		• next few weeks	• individual one-on-one support
			• referrals as required
		• next few months	• post incident education and preparation for next crisis

Obviously, all of the services which are described above can be considerably enhanced if an extensive program of preincident education exists within a community. Education before stress impact is one of the most important components of a systematic, comprehensive, and multicomponent approach to the management of stress in workplaces or in communities.

Effective intervention, as we have said many times before, depends heavily on the training and experience of the providers of help. We encourage everyone involved in Critical Incident Stress Management to obtain the proper training before engaging in any crisis intervention services.

APPENDIX C:

Psychoactive Stimulants Found in Over-the-Counter (OTC) Preparations

APPENDIX C:

Psychoactive Stimulants Found in
Over-the-Counter (OTC) Preparations

Dietary Substances:

Ma Huang

Kola Nut

Yohimbine

Gingko Biloba

Caffeine

Theobromine

Pharmaceuticals:

Ephedrine

Pseudoephedrine

Phenylpropanolamine

Phenylephrine Hydrochloride

APPENDIX D:

Common OTC Psychoactive Depressants

APPENDIX D

Common OTC Psychoactive Depressants

Alcohol
Nicotine
Antihistamines:
       Dimenhydrinate
       Diphenhydramine
       Promethazine
       Pyrathiazine

APPENDIX E:

Common Factors Increasing Suicidal Lethality

APPENDIX E

Common Factors Increasing Suicidal Lethality *

1. History of previous attempts
2. Family history of suicide or suicide attempts
3. Chronic pain or terminal illness
4. Financial or marital problems
5. Isolation, living alone
6. Hopelessness or helplessness
7. A detailed plan
8. Agitation
9. A psychiatric diagnosis or history of mental illness
10. Extreme guilt
11. Access to lethal means (e.g., guns, drugs)
12. Evidence of secondary gain associated with suicide (e.g., revenge, insurance, etc.)

*   Keep in mind, many suicides are actually accidental deaths where the suicide was intended to be only a gesture or manipulation

References

REFERENCES

American Academy of Orthopaedic Surgeons, Department of Research and Scientific Affairs. (1996). Tales from the Front: Huge response to sound off on CISD. *EMT Today*, Volume 1 (2), Feb / March 3.

American Psychiatric Association (1980). *Diagnostic and Statistical Manual of Mental Disorders, Third Ed.* Washington, D.C.: APA Press.

American Psychiatric Association (1994). *Diagnostic and Statistical Manual of Mental Disorders, Fourth Ed.* Washington, D.C.: APA Press.

American Red Cross (1991). *Disaster Mental Health Services (ARC 3050 M): Disaster Services Regulations and Procedures.* Alexandria, VA: Author.

Armstrong, K., O'Callahan, W. and Marmar, C. (1991). Debriefing Red Cross disaster personnel: The multiple stressor debriefing model. *Journal of Traumatic Stress*, 4, 581-593.

Backman, L., Arnetz, B., Levin, D., and Lublin, A. (1997). Psychophysiological effects of mental imaging training for police trainees. *Stress Medicine*, 13, 43-48.

Bandura, A. (1997). *Self-efficacy: The Exercise of Control.* NY: W.H. Freeman.

Beaton, R., Murphy, S. and Corneil, W (1996, September). Prevalence of posttraumatic stress disorder symptomatology in professional urban fire fighters in two countries. Paper presented to the International Congress of Occupational Health, Stockholm, Sweden.

Bettleheim, B. (1984). Afterward. In C. Vegh. *I Didn't Say Goodbye*. NY: E.P. Dutton

Bisson, J.I. and Deahl, M. (1994). Psychological debriefing and prevention of post-traumatic stress: More research is needed. *British Journal of Psychiatry*, 165, 717-720.

Blackwelder, N.L. (1995). *Critical Incident Stress Debriefing for School Employees*. Ann Arbor UMI Dissertation Services.

Bohl, N. (1991). The effectiveness of brief psychological interventions in police officers after critical incidents. In J.T. Reese, J. Horn, and C. Dunning (eds). *Critical Incidents in Policing*, Revised. Washington, D.C.: Department of Justice.

Bordow, S. and Porritt, D. (1979). An experimental evaluation of crisis intervention. *Social Science and Medicine*, 13, 251-256.

Bowlby, J. (1969). Attachment. NY: Basic Books.

British Psychological Working Party (1990). *Psychological Aspects of Disaster*. Leicester: British Psychological Society.

Brom, D., Kleber, R. and Hofman, M. (1993). Victims of traffic accidents: Incidence and prevention of post-traumatic stress disorder. *Journal of Clinical Psychology*, 49, 131 - 139.

Buckley, T.C., Blanchard, E. and Hickling, E. (1996) A prospective examination of delayed onset PTSD secondary to motor vehicle accidents. *Journal of Abnormal Psychology*, 105, 617-625.

Bunn, T. and Clarke, A. (1979). Crisis intervention. *British Journal of Medical Psychology*, 52, 191-195.

Burns, C. and Harm, I. (1993). Emergency nurses' perceptions of critical incidents and stress debriefings. *Journal of*

Emergency Nursing, 19, 431-436.

Caldwell, M.F. (1992). Incidence of PTSD among staff victims of patient violence. *Hospital and Community Psychiatry*, 8, 838 - 839.

Cal-OSHA (1994). *Guidelines for Workplace Security.* San Francisco, CA: Department of Industrial Relations.

Caplan, G. (1961). *An approach to Community Mental Health.* NY: Grune and Stratton.

Caplan, G. (1964). *Principles of Preventive Psychiatry.* NY: Basic Books.

Caplan, G. (1969). Opportunities for school psychologists in the primary prevention of mental health disorders in children. In A. Bindman and A. Spiegel (Eds.) *Perspectives in Community Mental Health* (pp. 420-436) Chicago: Aldine.

Chemtob, C.M., Thomas, S. Law,W. (1996). Post disaster psychological intervention: A field study of the impact of debriefing on psychological distress. Paper presented at the 2nd World Congress of the International Society Traumatic Stress Studies, June 9 - 13, 1996, Jerusalem.

Cohen, S. and Wills, T.A. (1985). Stress, social support, and the buffering hypothesis. *Psychological Bulletin*, 98, 310-357.

Corneil, D.W. (1993). *Prevalence of post-traumatic stress disorders in a metropolitan fire department.* Dissertation submitted to the School of Hygiene and Public Health, The Johns Hopkins University, Baltimore.

Dalgeish, T., Joseph, S., Thrasher, S., Tranah, T., and Yule, W. (1996) Crisis support following the Herald of Free Enterprise disaster. *Journal of Traumatic Stress*, 9, 833-845.

Deahl, M.P., Gillham, A., Thomas, J., Searle, M. and Srinivason (1994). Psychological sequelae following the Gulf War. *British Journal of Psychiatry*, 165, 60 - 65.

Department of Industrial Relations (1993). *Guidelines for Security and Safety of Health Care and Community Service Workers*. San Francisco: Author.

Dunning, C. (1988). Intervention strategies for emergency workers. In. M. Lystad (Ed). *Mental Health Response to Mass Emergencies* (pp. 284-310). NY: Brunner / Mazel.

Dyregrov, A. (1990). *Grief in Children*. London: Jessica Kingsley Publishers.

Everly, G.S. (1989). *A Clinical Guide to the Treatment of the Human Stress Response*. NY: Plenum.

Everly, G.S. (1993). Psychotraumatology: A two-factor formulation of posttraumatic stress. *Integrative Physiology and Behavioral Science* 28, 270-278.

Everly, G.S. (1993, October). Establishing a state-wide Red Cross disaster mental health network. Paper presented to the Annual Meeting of the International Society for Traumatic Stress Studies, San Antonio, TX.

Everly, G.S. (1995a). The role of the Critical Incident Stress Debriefing (CISD) process in disaster counseling. *Journal of Mental Health Counseling*, 17, 278-290.

Everly, G.S. (1995b). *A Psychological Trauma Prevention Program for the Kuwaiti Police*. Kuwait City: Social Development Office, Amiri Diwan.

Everly, G.S. (1996, February). The meaning of psychological trauma: An analysis of recurrent themes across cultures and settings. Invited paper presented to the Eighth Montreux Congress on Stress, Montreux, Switzerland.

Everly, G.S. (1997, Feb.) Critical Incident Stress Management: A proposed international standard of care for crisis intervention. Invited paper presented to the 9th Montreux Congress on Stress, Montreux, Switzerland.

Everly, G.S. and Lating, J. (1995) (Ed.). *Psychotraumatology: Key Papers and Core Concepts in Posttraumatic Stress.* NY: Plenum.

Everly, G.S., Mitchell, J., Schiller, G. (1995). Coldenham: Traumatic stress intervention in a community fire service. In G. Everly (Ed.) *Innovations in Disaster and Trauma Psychology, Volume I.* (pp. 238-245). Ellicott City, MD: Chevron Publishing Corporation.

Feldman, T.B. and Bell, R. (1991). Crisis debriefing of a jury after a murder trial. *Hospital and Community Psychiatry*, 42, 79-81.

Fernandez, N. (1994). *Operational Guide for the CISD Program.* Oakland, CA: Alameda County Mental Health Services.

Flanagan, J.C. (1954). The critical incident technique. *Psychological Bulletin*, 51, 327-358.

Flannery, R.B. (1990). Social Support and psychological trauma: A methodological review. *Journal of Traumatic Stress*, 3, 593-612.

Flannery, R.B., Fuleron, P., Trausch, J., and DeLoffi, A. (1991) A Program to help staff sope with psychological sequelae of assaults by patients. *Hospital and Community Psychiatry*, 42, 935 - 938.

Flannery, R.B., Hanson, M., Penk, W., Flannery, G. & Gallagher,

C. (1995). The Assaulted Staff Action Program: An approach to coping with the aftermath of violence in the workplace. In L. Murphy, J. Hurrell, S. Sauter, and G. Keita (Eds.). *Job Stress Interventions* (pp. 199-212). Washington, D.C.: APA Press.

Flannery, R.B. and Penk, W. (1996). Program evaluation of an intervention approach for staff assaulted by patients. Preliminary inquiry. *Journal of Traumatic Stress*, 9, 317 - 324.

Flannery, R.B., Penk, W., Hanson, M. (1995, September) The Assaulted staff action program (ASAP): A statewide replication. Paper presented to the APA/ NIOSH conference, Work, Stress and Health, '95, Washington, D.C.

Ford, J.D., Ruzek, J, and Niles, B. (1996). Identifying and treating VA medical care patients with undetected sequelae of psychological trauma and post-traumatic stress disorder. *NCP Clinical Quarterly*, 6, 77 - 82.

Frank, J.D. (1974). *Persuasion and Healing.* Baltimore: Johns Hopkins University Press.

Greenstone, J.C. (1993). *Critical Incident Stress Debriefing and Crisis Management.* Austin, TX: Texas Department of Health.

Hokanson, M. (1997). *Evaluation of the Effectiveness of the Critical Incident Stress Management Program for the Los Angeles County Fire Department.* Los Angeles: LACoFD.

Hytten, K. and Hasle, A. (1989). Fire-fighters: A study of stress and coping. *Acta Psychiatrica Scandinavica*, Supp. 355, 80, 50-55.

Jenkins, S.R. (1996). Social support and debriefing efficacy among emergency medical workers after a mass shooting incident. *Journal of Social Behavior and Personality,* 11, 477 - 492.

Jonsson, U. (1995). *Slutrapport Fran Globen-projektet.* Stockholm: Polishogskolan.

Kardiner, A. and Spiegel, H. (1947). *War, Stress, and Neurotic Illness.* NY: Hoeber.

Kenardy, J.A., Webster, R.A., Lewin, T.J., Carr, V.J., Hazell, P.L. and Carter, G.L. (1996) Stress debriefing and patterns of recovery following a natural disaster. *Journal of Traumatice Stress,* 9, 37 - 49.

Kennedy-Ewing, L. (1988). *Operational and Training Guide for the CISM Program of Delaware County, Pennsylvania.* Media, PA: Department of Human Resources.

Kessler, R.C., Sonnega, A., Bromet, E. Hughes, M., and Nelson, C. (1995). Posttraumatic stress disorder in the National Comorbidity Survey. *Archives of General Psychiatry,* 52, 1048 - 1060.

Kirwan, S. (1994) *Nursing Stress Pilot Project.* Winnipeg: Manitoba Provincial Medical Services.

Koss, M.P., Woodruff, W. and Koss, P.G. (1991). Criminal victimization among primary care medical patients. *Behavioral Sciences and the Law,* 9, 85 - 46.

Leeman-Conley. (1990). After a violent robbery ... *Criminology Australia,* April / May, 4-6.

Lindemann, E. (1994). Symptomatology and management of acute grief. *American Journal of Psychiatry,* 101, 141-148.

Lindy, J.D. (1985). The trauma membrane and other clinical concepts derived from psychotherapeutic work with survivors of natural disaster. *Psychiatric Annals*, 15, 153-160.

McFarlane, A.C. (1988). The longitudinal course of posttraumatic morbidity. *Journal of Nervous and Mental Disease*, 176, 30 - 39.

Manton, M. and Talbot, A. (1990). Crisis intervention after an armed hold-up. *Journal of Traumatic Stress*, 3, 507-522.

Manzi, L.A. (1995). *Evaluation of the On Site Academy's Residential Program.* Research investigation submitted to Boston College.

Martinez, E. (1995). CIRP reduces stress. *Airline Pilot*, 64, 30-34, 61.

Maslow, A. (1970). *Motivation and Personality.* NY: Harper and Row.

Meehan, D. (1996) Critical Incident Stress Debriefing. *Navy Medicine*, 35, 4-7.

Mitchell, J.T. (1983a) When disaster strikes...The critical incident stress debriefing process. *Journal of Emergency Medical Services*, 8, 36-39.

Mitchell, J.T. (1983b). Guidelines for psychological debriefings. *Emergency Management Course Manual.* Emmitsburg, MD: Federal Emergency Management Agency, Emergency Management Institute.

Mitchell, J.T. (1988a). The history, status, and future of critical incident stress debriefings. *Journal of Emergency Medical Services*, 13, (11), 49-52.

Mitchell, J.T. (1988b). Development and functions of a critical incident stress debriefing team. *Journal of Emergency Medical Services*, 13, (12), 43-46.

Mitchell, J.T. and Everly, G. (1993). *Human Elements Training in Emergency Services*. Ellicott City, MD: Chevron Publishing Corporation.

Mitchell, J.T. and Everly, G. (1996). *Critical Incident Stress Debriefing: An Operations Manual for the Prevention of Traumatic Stress Among Emergency Services and Disaster Workers*. Ellicott City, MD: Chevron Publishing Corporation.

Mitchell, J.T. and Everly, G.S. (1997). Scientific evidence for Critical Incident Stress Management. *Journal of Emergency Medical Services*, 22, 87 - 93.

Myers, D. (1995). Worker stress during longterm disaster recovery efforts. In G. Everly (Ed.) *Innovations in Disaster and Trauma Psychology, Volume one* (pp. 158-191). Ellicott City, MD: Chevron Publishing Corporation.

Neil, T., Oney, J. DiFonso, L., Thacker, B., and Reichart, W. (1974). *Emotional First Aid*. Louisville: Kemper-Behavioral Science Associates.

NIOSH. (1996). *Current Intelligence Bulletin 57: Violence in the Workplace*. Washington, D.C.: Author.

OSHA. (1996). *Guidelines for Preventing Workplace Violence for Health Care and Social Service Workers* - OSHA 3148 1996. Washington, D.C.: Author.

Parad, H. (1996). The use of time limited crisis intervention in community mental health programming. *Social Service Review*, 40, 275-282.

Pennebaker, J.W. (1985). Traumatic experience and psychosomatic disease. *Canadian Psychologist*, 26, 82-95.

Pennebaker, J.W. (1990). *Opening Up: The Healing Power of Confiding in Others*. NY: Avon.

Pennebaker, J.W. and Beall, S. (1986). Confronting a traumatic event. *Journal of Abnormal Psychology*, 95, 274-281.

Post, R. (1992). Transduction of psychosocial stress onto the neurobiology of recurrent affective disorder. *American Journal of Psychiatry*, 149-990-1010.

Raphael, B. (1986). *When Disaster Strikes*. NY: Basic Books.

Rapoport, L. (1965). The state of crisis. Some theoretical considerations. In H. Parad (Ed) *Crisis Intervention: Selected Readings* (pp. 22-31). NY: Family Service Association of America.

Rayner, S. (1994). *Royal Australian Navy CISM Operating Manual*. Canberra: Naval Personnel Services.

Robinson, R. (1995). Critical Incident Stress Management in Australia. In G. Everly (Ed.) *Innovations in Disaster and Trauma Psychology, Volume I* (pp. 90-106). Ellicott City, MD: Chevron Publishing Corporation.

Robinson, R.C. and Mitchell, J.T. (1993). Evaluation of psychological debriefings. *Journal of TraumaticStress, 6(3), 367 - 382.*

Robinson, R.C. and Mitchell, J.T. (1995). Getting Some Balance Back into the Debriefing Debate. *The Bulletin of the Australian Psychological Society,* vol. 17 (10), 5 - 10.

Rogers, C. (1951). *Client-centered Therapy.* Boston: Houghton Mifflin.

Rogers, O.W. (1993). *An examination of Critical Incident Stress Debriefing for Emergency Services Providers: A quasi experimental field study.* Ann Arbor, MI: UMI Dissertation Services.

Salmon, T.W. (1919). War neuroses and their lesson. *New York Medical Journal,* 109, 993-994.

Seligman, M.E.P. (1995). The effectiveness of psychotherapy. *American Psychologist,* vol. 29, (12), 965 - 974.

Slaby, A., Lieb, J., and Tancredi, L. (1975) *Handbook of Psychiatric Emergencies.* Flushing, NY: Medical Examination Publishing.

Solomon, R, (1995). Critical incident stress management in law enforcement. In G. Everly (Ed.) *Innovations in Disaster and Trauma Psychology, Volume I* (pp. 123-157). Ellicott City, MD: Chevron Publishing Corporation.

Solomon, Z. and Benbenishty, R. (1986). The role of proximity, immediacy, and expectancy in frontline treatment of combat stress reaction among Israelis in the Lebanon War. *American Journal of Psychiatry,* 143, 613-617.

Spiegel, D. and Classen, C. (1995). Acute stress disorder. In G. Gabbard (Ed.). *Treatments of Psychiatric Disorders* (pp. 1521-1537). Washington, D.C.: American Psychiatric Press.

Spitzer, W. J. and Burke, L. (1993). A critical incident stress debriefing program for hospital-based health care personnel. *Health and Social Work,* 18, 149-156.

Stallard, P. and Law, F. (1993). Screening and psychological debriefing of adolescent survivors of life threatening events. *British Journal of Psychiatry*, 163, 660-665.

Stierlin, E. (1909). *Psycho-neuropathology as a Result of a Mining Disaster March 10, 1906*. Zurich: University of Zurich.

Strub, R.L. and Black, F.W. (1993). *The Mental Status Examination in Neurology, Third Edition*. Philadelphia: F.A. Davis.

Talbot, A., Manton, M., and Dunn, P, (1992). Debriefing the debriefers. *Journal of Traumatic Stress*, 5, 45-62.

Taylor, S. (1983). Adjustment to threatening events. *American Psychologist*, 38, 1161-1173.

U.S. Air Force (1996). *Critical Incident Stress Management*. Author.

van der Hart, O. Brown, P., and van der Kolk, B. (1989). Pierre Janet's treatment of posttraumatic stress. *Journal of Traumatic Stress*, 2,379-396.

Van Goethem, R. (1989). *CISD Training Document* Alberta: Access Network.

Violanti, J.M. (1996). Police suicide: Risks and relationships. *Frontline Counselor*, 4, 6.

Wee, D. (1996). Research in Critical Incident Stress Management, Part 4, How effective is this? *Life Net 7* (2) p. 4-5.

Wee, D.F., Mills, D.M. and Koelher, G. (1993). Stress response of emergency medical services personnel following the Los Angeles civil disturbances. In G. Koelher, et al.*Medical Care for the the injured: The emergency medical response to the April 1992 Los Angeles Civil Disturbance*. (EMSA

393 - 01). Sacramento, CA: Emergency Medical Authority.

Weis, D.S., Marmar, C., Metzler, T. and Ronfeldt, H. (1995). Predicting symptomatic distress in emergency services personnel. *Journal of Consulting and Clinical Psychology*, 63, 361 - 368.

Weisaeth, L. (1989). A study of behavioural responses to an industrial disaster. *Acta Psychiatrica Scandinavica*, Supp. 355, 80, 13-24.

Welzant, V., Torpey, R., Sienkilewski, K. (1995). Developing a critical incident stress debriefing team in a mental health care system. *Journal of the American Psychiatric Nurses Association*, 1, 177-181.

Western Management Consultants. (1996). *The Medical Services Branch CISM Evaluation Report*. Vancouver, B.C.: Author.

Wollman, D. (1993). Critical incident stress debriefing and crisis groups: A review of literature. *Group*, 17, 70-83.

Yalom, I. (1970). *Theory and Practice of Group Psychotherapy*. NY: Basic books.

Ziegler, J.S. (1992, Aug). Actuarial prediction of violence in a psychiatric population. Paper presented to the 100th Annual Convention of the American Psychological Association, Washington, D.C.

Index